MW01234063

INDEX

Page numbers in *italics* denote tables, those in **bold** denote figures.

Taylor & Francis

eBooks

FOR LIBRARIES

ORDER YOUR FREE 30 DAY INSTITUTIONAL TRIAL TODAY!

Over 23,000 eBook titles in the Humanities, Social Sciences, STM and Law from some of the world's leading imprints.

Choose from a range of subject packages or create your own!

Benefits for you

▶ Free MARC records

▶ COUNTER-compliant usage statistics

▶ Flexible purchase and pricing options

Benefits for your user

▶ Off-site, anytime access via Athens or referring URL

▶ Print or copy pages or chapters

▶ Full content search

▶ Bookmark, highlight and annotate text

▶ Access to thousands of pages of quality research at the click of a button

For more information, pricing enquiries or to order a free trial, contact your local online sales team.

UK and Rest of World: **online.sales@tandf.co.uk**

US, Canada and Latin America:
e-reference@taylorandfrancis.com

www.ebooksubscriptions.com

ALPSP Award for BEST eBOOK PUBLISHER 2009 Finalist

Taylor & Francis eBooks
Taylor & Francis Group

A flexible and dynamic resource for teaching, learning and research.

Made in the USA
Las Vegas, NV
19 August 2024

94070104R00201

Our
Kitchen Aid
Ice Cream Maker Attachment
Cookbook

Jessie Mohr

Copyright © 2024 by Jessie Mohr

All rights reserved. The content contained within this book may not be reproduced, duplicated or transmitted without direct written permission from the author or the publisher.

Legal Notice:

This book is copyright protected. This book is only for personal use. You cannot amend, distribute, sell, use, quote or paraphrase any part, or the content within this book, without the consent of the author or publisher.

Disclaimer Notice:

Please note the information contained within this document is for educational and entertainment purposes only. All effort has been executed to present accurate, up to date, and reliable, complete information. No warranties of any kind are declared or implied. Readers acknowledge that the author is not engaging in the rendering of legal, financial, medical or professional advice.

The content within this book has been derived from various sources. Please consult a licensed professional before attempting any techniques outlined in this book.

By reading this document, the reader agrees that under no circumstances is the author responsible for any losses, direct or indirect, which are incurred as a result of the use of information contained within this document, including, but not limited to, – errors, omissions, or inaccuracies.

Acknowledgments

I would like to thank the dedicated team of recipe developers, testers, and editors who contributed to this book. Special thanks to KitchenAid for their innovative products and to my families and friends for their encouragement.

Contents

Introduction

While there are countless varieties and flavors to enjoy, creating your own ice cream at home hasn't always been an easy task. Traditional hand-crank ice cream makers were large, cumbersome, and difficult to store. The process of making ice cream manually was laborious and time-consuming, often requiring at least three strong individuals to operate.

First, you had to prepare a custard mixture, which then needed to chill overnight. Next, you had to assemble the machine, add rock salt and ice outside the vessel, which was both messy and challenging. Once the custard mixture was added, you had to crank the handle until the ice cream froze. During this process, it was necessary to add more rock salt and ice as they melted, ensure the salt didn't get into the ice cream, and monitor the paddle to prevent the ice cream from hardening too much. After all this effort, the churned ice cream had to "ripen" in the freezer for at least eight hours before it could be served. While the results were delicious, the arduous process often made store-bought ice cream a more convenient option, despite the limited flavor choices.

The advent of electric ice cream makers simplified the process but introduced new challenges. The early models were so noisy that many families preferred to operate them outside, much to the annoyance of their neighbors. Ironically, these electric machines were just as bulky as their hand-cranked predecessors and still required the use of rock salt and ice, making them only marginally more convenient.

Introducing the KitchenAid Ice Cream Maker Attachment, a revolutionary tool for homemade ice cream. This attachment integrates effortlessly with your KitchenAid stand mixer, removing the need for rock salt and ice. It provides a more efficient and user-friendly ice cream-making experience. With the KitchenAid Ice Cream Attachment, you can create smooth, creamy, and delicious ice cream in just 20-30 minutes, without the noise and bulk associated with traditional electric ice cream makers.

1. Getting Started

Essential Tools and Ingredients

To create the perfect homemade ice cream with your KitchenAid Ice Cream Maker Attachment, you'll need a few essential tools and ingredients. Here's a guide to help you get started:

Essential Tools

KitchenAid Stand Mixer: The foundation for your ice cream maker attachment. Ensure your stand mixer is compatible with the attachment.

KitchenAid Ice Cream Maker Attachment: This includes the freeze bowl, dasher, and drive assembly.

Mixing Bowls: For preparing and mixing your ice cream base ingredients.

Whisk or Electric Mixer: To thoroughly combine your ingredients.

Spatula: For scraping down the sides of the mixing bowl and transferring the ice cream to the freeze bowl.

Measuring Cups and Spoons: Accurate measurements are key to perfect ice cream.

Freezer-Safe Containers: For storing your churned ice cream.

Timer: To keep track of the churning time.

Plastic Wrap or Parchment Paper: To cover the surface of the ice cream in the container, preventing ice crystals from forming.

Essential Ingredients

Dairy: Heavy cream, whole milk, and sometimes half-and-half are the base for most ice creams, providing richness and creaminess.

Sugar: Granulated sugar is commonly used to sweeten the ice cream.

Egg Yolks: Used in custard-based ice creams for added richness and a smooth texture.

Vanilla Extract: A primary flavoring for classic vanilla ice cream and a base for many other flavors.

Salt: A small amount enhances the overall flavor and balances sweetness.

Flavorings and Add-Ins: Fresh fruits, chocolate chips, nuts, cookies, caramel, and other ingredients to create unique and delicious flavors.

Non-Dairy Alternatives: Coconut milk, almond milk, and other plant-based milks for dairy-free and vegan ice creams.

Stabilizers: Corn syrup or gelatin can help improve the texture and prevent ice crystals.

Preparing Your Ingredients

Chill Your Ingredients: For the smoothest ice cream, ensure all your ingredients are well-chilled before mixing. This helps the ice cream freeze faster and reduces the formation of ice crystals.

Pre-Freeze the Bowl: The KitchenAid freeze bowl must be completely frozen before use. This usually takes 15-24 hours, so plan accordingly.

Prep Your Add-Ins: Chop fruits, nuts, or other mix-ins into small pieces so they can be evenly distributed throughout the ice cream.

Basic Techniques for Making Ice Cream

Creating delicious homemade ice cream with your KitchenAid Ice Cream Maker Attachment is a straightforward process, but mastering a few basic techniques will help you achieve the best results. Here's a guide to help you get started:

Preparing the Freeze Bowl

Freeze the Bowl in Advance: Place the KitchenAid freeze bowl in your freezer at least 15-24 hours before you plan to make ice cream. The bowl should be completely frozen to ensure proper churning.

Test for Readiness: Shake the freeze bowl; if you do not hear any liquid moving inside, it is fully frozen and ready to use.

Making the Ice Cream Base

Custard Base: For a rich, creamy texture, many ice cream recipes use a custard base made from dairy, sugar, and egg yolks.

Heat the Dairy: In a saucepan, heat the cream and milk until it begins to steam but not boil.

Whisk the Yolks and Sugar: In a separate bowl, whisk egg yolks with sugar until pale and thick.

Temper the Eggs: Gradually add the hot dairy mixture to the egg mixture, whisking constantly to prevent the eggs from curdling.

Cook the Custard: Return the mixture to the saucepan and cook over low heat, stirring constantly, until it thickens enough to coat the back of a spoon.

Chill the Base: Strain the custard through a fine-mesh sieve into a bowl, cover, and chill in the refrigerator for several hours or overnight.

Philadelphia-Style Base: This base skips the eggs and is quicker to prepare, resulting in a lighter texture.

Mix the Ingredients: Combine cream, milk, sugar, and flavorings (such as vanilla) in a bowl and whisk until the sugar is dissolved.

Chill the Base: Cover and refrigerate until well chilled, at least an hour.

Churning the Ice Cream

Set Up the Mixer: Attach the frozen freeze bowl to your KitchenAid stand mixer and attach the dasher and drive assembly.

Start the Mixer: Turn the mixer to the "stir" or low setting before pouring in your ice cream base to prevent splashing.

Pour in the Base: Slowly pour the chilled ice cream base into the freeze bowl while the mixer is running.

Churn: Allow the mixer to churn the ice cream for 20-30 minutes. The mixture will start to thicken and resemble soft-serve ice cream.

Add Mix-Ins: If you're adding any mix-ins like chocolate chips, nuts, or fruit, add them during the last few minutes of churning.

Hardening the Ice Cream

Transfer to a Container: Use a spatula to transfer the churned ice cream to a freezer-safe container.

Cover the Ice Cream: Place a piece of plastic wrap or parchment paper directly on the surface of the ice cream to prevent ice crystals from forming.

Freeze: Place the container in the freezer for at least 2 hours, or until the ice cream is firm.

Serving and Storing

Scoop and Serve: Let the ice cream sit at room temperature for a few minutes to soften slightly before scooping.

Store Properly: Keep the ice cream covered in the freezer to maintain its texture and prevent freezer burn. Homemade ice cream is best enjoyed within a week for optimal freshness and flavor.

Care and Maintenance

Cleaning: Wash the freeze bowl, dasher, and drive assembly with warm, soapy water. Do not use abrasive cleaners or scouring pads.

Storage: After cleaning, thoroughly dry the freeze bowl before storing it in the freezer or a cool, dry place.

Inspection: Regularly inspect the attachment parts for wear and tear. Replace any damaged components to ensure optimal performance.

Troubleshooting Tips

Ice Cream is Too Soft: Ensure the freeze bowl was properly frozen, and the base was adequately chilled before churning.

Ice Crystals Forming: Make sure to cover the surface of the ice cream with plastic wrap or parchment paper before freezing.

Base Not Thickening: If making a custard base, ensure it is cooked to the right consistency. If the base is too thin, the final ice cream will not be as creamy.

2. Classic Ice Creams

Vanilla Ice Cream

Servings: 8

Ingredients

- 2 cups heavy cream
- 2 cups whole milk
- 1 cup granulated sugar
- 2 teaspoons pure vanilla extract
- Pinch of salt

Instructions

In a medium bowl, whisk together the heavy cream, whole milk, sugar, vanilla extract, and salt until the sugar is completely dissolved.

Pour the mixture into the KitchenAid Ice Cream Attachment.

Churn on low speed for 20-25 minutes, or until the mixture reaches a soft-serve consistency.

Transfer the ice cream to a lidded container and freeze for at least 2 hours before serving.

Chocolate Ice Cream

Servings: 8

Ingredients

- 2 cups heavy cream
- 2 cups whole milk
- 1 cup granulated sugar

- 3/4 cup unsweetened cocoa powder
- 1 teaspoon pure vanilla extract
- Pinch of salt

Instructions

In a medium bowl, whisk together the heavy cream, whole milk, sugar, cocoa powder, vanilla extract, and salt until the sugar and cocoa are completely dissolved.

Pour the mixture into the KitchenAid Ice Cream Attachment.

Churn on low speed for 20-25 minutes, or until the mixture reaches a soft-serve consistency.

Transfer the ice cream to a lidded container and freeze for at least 2 hours before serving.

Strawberry Ice Cream

Servings: 8

Ingredients

- 2 cups fresh strawberries, hulled and chopped
- 2 cups heavy cream
- 2 cups whole milk
- 1 cup granulated sugar
- 2 teaspoons lemon juice
- 1 teaspoon pure vanilla extract
- Pinch of salt

Instructions

In a blender or food processor, puree the strawberries until smooth.

In a medium bowl, whisk together the strawberry puree, heavy cream, whole milk, sugar, lemon juice, vanilla extract, and salt until the sugar is completely dissolved.

Pour the mixture into the KitchenAid Ice Cream Attachment.

Churn on low speed for 20-25 minutes, or until the mixture reaches a soft-serve consistency.

Transfer the ice cream to a lidded container and freeze for at least 2 hours before serving.

Mint Chocolate Chip Ice Cream

Servings: 8

Ingredients

- 2 cups heavy cream
- 2 cups whole milk
- 1 cup granulated sugar
- 2 teaspoons pure mint extract
- Pinch of salt
- 1 cup mini chocolate chips

Instructions

In a medium bowl, whisk together the heavy cream, whole milk, sugar, mint extract, and salt until the sugar is completely dissolved.

Pour the mixture into the KitchenAid Ice Cream Attachment.

Churn on low speed for 15-20 minutes, then add the mini chocolate chips.

Continue churning for an additional 5-10 minutes, or until the mixture reaches a soft-serve consistency.

Transfer the ice cream to a lidded container and freeze for at least 2 hours before serving.

Cookies and Cream Ice Cream

Servings: 8

Ingredients

- 2 cups heavy cream
- 2 cups whole milk
- 1 cup granulated sugar
- 2 teaspoons pure vanilla extract
- Pinch of salt
- 1 cup crushed chocolate sandwich cookies (such as Oreos)

Instructions

In a medium bowl, whisk together the heavy cream, whole milk, sugar, vanilla extract, and salt until the sugar is completely dissolved.

Pour the mixture into the KitchenAid Ice Cream Attachment.

Churn on low speed for 15-20 minutes, then add the crushed cookies.

Continue churning for an additional 5-10 minutes, or until the mixture reaches a soft-serve consistency.

Transfer the ice cream to a lidded container and freeze for at least 2 hours before serving.

Salted Caramel Ice Cream

Servings: 8

Ingredients

- 2 cups heavy cream
- 2 cups whole milk
- 1 cup granulated sugar
- 1/2 cup caramel sauce (homemade or store-bought)

- 1 teaspoon sea salt
- 1 teaspoon pure vanilla extract

Instructions

In a medium bowl, whisk together the heavy cream, whole milk, sugar, caramel sauce, sea salt, and vanilla extract until the sugar is completely dissolved.

Pour the mixture into the KitchenAid Ice Cream Attachment.

Churn on low speed for 20-25 minutes, or until the mixture reaches a soft-serve consistency.

Transfer the ice cream to a lidded container and freeze for at least 2 hours before serving.

Honey Lavender Ice Cream

Servings: 8

Ingredients

- 2 cups heavy cream
- 2 cups whole milk
- 1 cup granulated sugar
- 1/4 cup honey
- 1 tablespoon dried culinary lavender
- 1 teaspoon pure vanilla extract
- Pinch of salt

Instructions

In a saucepan, combine the heavy cream, whole milk, sugar, honey, and lavender. Heat over medium heat until the mixture is hot but not boiling, stirring occasionally. Remove from heat and let steep for 15 minutes.

Strain the mixture through a fine-mesh sieve to remove the lavender.

Add the vanilla extract and salt, and whisk until combined.

Chill the mixture in the refrigerator until completely cool.

Pour the mixture into the KitchenAid Ice Cream Attachment.

Churn on low speed for 20-25 minutes, or until the mixture reaches a soft-serve consistency.

Transfer the ice cream to a lidded container and freeze for at least 2 hours before serving.

Pistachio Ice Cream

Servings: 8

Ingredients

- 2 cups heavy cream
- 2 cups whole milk
- 1 cup granulated sugar
- 1/2 cup finely chopped pistachios
- 1 teaspoon pure vanilla extract
- 1/2 teaspoon almond extract
- Pinch of salt

Instructions

In a medium bowl, whisk together the heavy cream, whole milk, sugar, chopped pistachios, vanilla extract, almond extract, and salt until the sugar is completely dissolved.

Pour the mixture into the KitchenAid Ice Cream Attachment.

Churn on low speed for 20-25 minutes, or until the mixture reaches a soft-serve consistency.

Transfer the ice cream to a lidded container and freeze for at least 2 hours before serving.

Black Sesame Ice Cream

Servings: 8

Ingredients

- 2 cups heavy cream
- 2 cups whole milk
- 1 cup granulated sugar
- 1/2 cup black sesame paste
- 1 teaspoon pure vanilla extract
- Pinch of salt

Instructions

In a medium bowl, whisk together the heavy cream, whole milk, sugar, black sesame paste, vanilla extract, and salt until the sugar is completely dissolved.

Pour the mixture into the KitchenAid Ice Cream Attachment.

Churn on low speed for 20-25 minutes, or until the mixture reaches a soft-serve consistency.

Transfer the ice cream to a lidded container and freeze for at least 2 hours before serving.

Earl Grey Ice Cream

Servings: 8

Ingredients

- 2 cups heavy cream
- 2 cups whole milk
- 1 cup granulated sugar
- 4 Earl Grey tea bags
- 1 teaspoon pure vanilla extract
- Pinch of salt

Instructions

In a saucepan, combine the heavy cream and whole milk. Heat over medium heat until the mixture is hot but not boiling.

Remove from heat, add the tea bags, and let steep for 10 minutes. Remove the tea bags, squeezing out any excess liquid.

Whisk in the sugar, vanilla extract, and salt until the sugar is completely dissolved.

Chill the mixture in the refrigerator until completely cool.

Pour the mixture into the KitchenAid Ice Cream Attachment.

Churn on low speed for 20-25 minutes, or until the mixture reaches a soft-serve consistency.

Transfer the ice cream to a lidded container and freeze for at least 2 hours before serving.

Coffee Ice Cream

Servings: 8

Ingredients

- 2 cups heavy cream
- 2 cups whole milk
- 1 cup granulated sugar
- 3 tablespoons instant coffee granules
- 1 teaspoon pure vanilla extract
- Pinch of salt

Instructions

In a medium bowl, whisk together the heavy cream, whole milk, sugar, coffee granules, vanilla extract, and salt until the sugar and coffee granules are completely dissolved.

Pour the mixture into the KitchenAid Ice Cream Attachment.

Churn on low speed for 20-25 minutes, or until the mixture reaches a soft-serve consistency.

Transfer the ice cream to a lidded container and freeze for at least 2 hours before serving.

Banana Ice Cream

Servings: 8

Ingredients

- 3 ripe bananas, mashed
- 2 cups heavy cream
- 2 cups whole milk
- 3/4 cup granulated sugar
- 1 teaspoon pure vanilla extract
- Pinch of salt

Instructions

In a medium bowl, whisk together the mashed bananas, heavy cream, whole milk, sugar, vanilla extract, and salt until the sugar is completely dissolved.

Pour the mixture into the KitchenAid Ice Cream Attachment.

Churn on low speed for 20-25 minutes, or until the mixture reaches a soft-serve consistency.

Transfer the ice cream to a lidded container and freeze for at least 2 hours before serving.

Butter Pecan Ice Cream

Servings: 8

Ingredients

- 1 cup pecan halves, chopped
- 2 tablespoons unsalted butter
- 2 cups heavy cream
- 2 cups whole milk
- 1 cup brown sugar
- 1 teaspoon pure vanilla extract
- Pinch of salt

Instructions

In a skillet, melt the butter over medium heat. Add the pecans and cook, stirring frequently, until the pecans are lightly toasted, about 5 minutes. Remove from heat and let cool.

In a medium bowl, whisk together the heavy cream, whole milk, brown sugar, vanilla extract, and salt until the sugar is completely dissolved. Stir in the toasted pecans.

Pour the mixture into the KitchenAid Ice Cream Attachment.

Churn on low speed for 20-25 minutes, or until the mixture reaches a soft-serve consistency.

Transfer the ice cream to a lidded container and freeze for at least 2 hours before serving.

Coconut Ice Cream

Servings: 8

Ingredients

- 2 cups coconut milk
- 2 cups heavy cream
- 1 cup granulated sugar
- 1 teaspoon pure vanilla extract
- Pinch of salt
- 1/2 cup shredded coconut (optional)

Instructions

In a medium bowl, whisk together the coconut milk, heavy cream, sugar, vanilla extract, and salt until the sugar is completely dissolved.

Stir in the shredded coconut if using.

Pour the mixture into the KitchenAid Ice Cream Attachment.

Churn on low speed for 20-25 minutes, or until the mixture reaches a soft-serve consistency.

Transfer the ice cream to a lidded container and freeze for at least 2 hours before serving.

Peach Ice Cream

Servings: 8

Ingredients

- 3 ripe peaches, peeled and chopped
- 2 cups heavy cream
- 2 cups whole milk
- 1 cup granulated sugar
- 2 teaspoons lemon juice
- 1 teaspoon pure vanilla extract
- Pinch of salt

Instructions

In a blender or food processor, puree the peaches until smooth.

In a medium bowl, whisk together the peach puree, heavy cream, whole milk, sugar, lemon juice, vanilla extract, and salt until the sugar is completely dissolved.

Pour the mixture into the KitchenAid Ice Cream Attachment.

Churn on low speed for 20-25 minutes, or until the mixture reaches a soft-serve consistency.

Transfer the ice cream to a lidded container and freeze for at least 2 hours before serving.

Peanut Butter Ice Cream

Servings: 8

Ingredients

- 2 cups heavy cream
- 2 cups whole milk
- 1 cup granulated sugar
- 3/4 cup creamy peanut butter
- 1 teaspoon pure vanilla extract
- Pinch of salt

Instructions

In a medium bowl, whisk together the heavy cream, whole milk, sugar, peanut butter, vanilla extract, and salt until the sugar is completely dissolved and the peanut butter is well incorporated.

Pour the mixture into the KitchenAid Ice Cream Attachment.

Churn on low speed for 20-25 minutes, or until the mixture reaches a soft-serve consistency.

Transfer the ice cream to a lidded container and freeze for at least 2 hours before serving.

Maple Walnut Ice Cream

Servings: 8

Ingredients

- 2 cups heavy cream
- 2 cups whole milk
- 1 cup maple syrup
- 1 cup chopped walnuts
- 1 teaspoon pure vanilla extract
- Pinch of salt

Instructions

In a medium bowl, whisk together the heavy cream, whole milk, maple syrup, vanilla extract, and salt until well combined.

Stir in the chopped walnuts.

Pour the mixture into the KitchenAid Ice Cream Attachment.

Churn on low speed for 20-25 minutes, or until the mixture reaches a soft-serve consistency.

Transfer the ice cream to a lidded container and freeze for at least 2 hours before serving.

Lemon Ice Cream

Servings: 8

Ingredients

- 2 cups heavy cream
- 2 cups whole milk
- 1 cup granulated sugar
- 1/2 cup fresh lemon juice
- 1 tablespoon lemon zest
- 1 teaspoon pure vanilla extract
- Pinch of salt

Instructions

In a medium bowl, whisk together the heavy cream, whole milk, sugar, lemon juice, lemon zest, vanilla extract, and salt until the sugar is completely dissolved.

Pour the mixture into the KitchenAid Ice Cream Attachment.

Churn on low speed for 20-25 minutes, or until the mixture reaches a soft-serve consistency.

Transfer the ice cream to a lidded container and freeze for at least 2 hours before serving.

Blueberry Ice Cream

Servings: 8

Ingredients

- 2 cups fresh blueberries
- 2 cups heavy cream
- 2 cups whole milk
- 1 cup granulated sugar
- 2 teaspoons lemon juice
- 1 teaspoon pure vanilla extract
- Pinch of salt

Instructions

In a blender or food processor, puree the blueberries until smooth.

In a medium bowl, whisk together the blueberry puree, heavy cream, whole milk, sugar, lemon juice, vanilla extract, and salt until the sugar is completely dissolved.

Pour the mixture into the KitchenAid Ice Cream Attachment.

Churn on low speed for 20-25 minutes, or until the mixture reaches a soft-serve consistency.

Transfer the ice cream to a lidded container and freeze for at least 2 hours before serving.

Mango Ice Cream

Servings: 8

Ingredients

- 2 ripe mangoes, peeled and chopped
- 2 cups heavy cream
- 2 cups whole milk
- 1 cup granulated sugar
- 2 teaspoons lemon juice
- 1 teaspoon pure vanilla extract
- Pinch of salt

Instructions

In a blender or food processor, puree the mangoes until smooth.

In a medium bowl, whisk together the mango puree, heavy cream, whole milk, sugar, lemon juice, vanilla extract, and salt until the sugar is completely dissolved.

Pour the mixture into the KitchenAid Ice Cream Attachment.

Churn on low speed for 20-25 minutes, or until the mixture reaches a soft-serve consistency.

Transfer the ice cream to a lidded container and freeze for at least 2 hours before serving.

3. Gourmet Ice Creams

Dulce de Leche Ice Cream

Servings: 8

Ingredients

- 2 cups heavy cream
- 1 cup whole milk
- 3/4 cup granulated sugar
- 1 cup dulce de leche
- 1 teaspoon pure vanilla extract

Instructions

In a medium bowl, whisk together the cream, milk, sugar, dulce de leche, and vanilla extract until the sugar is completely dissolved and the mixture is smooth.

Pour the mixture into the KitchenAid Ice Cream Attachment.

Churn on low speed for 25-30 minutes, or until the mixture reaches a soft-serve consistency.

Transfer the ice cream to a lidded container and freeze for at least 2 hours before serving.

Coconut Lemongrass Ice Cream

Servings: 8

Ingredients

- 2 cups coconut milk
- 1 cup heavy cream
- 3/4 cup granulated sugar
- 2 stalks lemongrass, finely chopped
- 1 tablespoon fresh lime zest
- 1 teaspoon pure vanilla extract

Instructions

In a medium saucepan, combine the coconut milk, heavy cream, sugar, lemongrass, and lime zest. Heat over medium heat until it just starts to simmer, then remove from heat and let steep for 30 minutes. Strain to remove lemongrass pieces.

Whisk in the vanilla extract.

Pour the mixture into the KitchenAid Ice Cream Attachment.

Churn on low speed for 25-30 minutes, or until the mixture reaches a soft-serve consistency.

Transfer the ice cream to a lidded container and freeze for at least 2 hours before serving.

Tiramisu Ice Cream

Servings: 8

Ingredients

- 2 cups heavy cream
- 1 cup whole milk
- 3/4 cup granulated sugar
- 1/2 cup mascarpone cheese
- 1/4 cup brewed espresso, cooled

- 1/4 cup coffee liqueur
- 1 teaspoon pure vanilla extract
- 1/2 cup ladyfinger cookies, crumbled
- 1 tablespoon cocoa powder

Instructions

In a medium bowl, whisk together the cream, milk, sugar, mascarpone, espresso, coffee liqueur, and vanilla extract until smooth and the sugar is dissolved.

Pour the mixture into the KitchenAid Ice Cream Attachment.

Churn on low speed for 25-30 minutes, or until the mixture reaches a soft-serve consistency.

In the last 5 minutes of churning, add the crumbled ladyfingers.

Transfer the ice cream to a lidded container and freeze for at least 2 hours before serving. Dust with cocoa powder before serving.

Mango Lassi Ice Cream

Servings: 8

Ingredients

- 2 cups ripe mango puree (about 2 large mangoes)
- 1 cup plain yogurt
- 1 cup heavy cream
- 3/4 cup granulated sugar
- 1 teaspoon cardamom powder
- 1 teaspoon pure vanilla extract

Instructions

In a blender, combine the mango puree, yogurt, cream, sugar, cardamom, and vanilla extract. Blend until smooth.

Pour the mixture into the KitchenAid Ice Cream Attachment.

Churn on low speed for 25-30 minutes, or until the mixture reaches a soft-serve consistency.

Transfer the ice cream to a lidded container and freeze for at least 2 hours before serving.

Açai Berry Ice Cream

Servings: 8

Ingredients

- 2 cups açai berry puree
- 1 cup heavy cream
- 1 cup whole milk
- 3/4 cup granulated sugar
- 1 teaspoon pure vanilla extract

Instructions

In a medium bowl, whisk together the açai puree, cream, milk, sugar, and vanilla extract until the sugar is completely dissolved.

Pour the mixture into the KitchenAid Ice Cream Attachment.

Churn on low speed for 25-30 minutes, or until the mixture reaches a soft-serve consistency.

Transfer the ice cream to a lidded container and freeze for at least 2 hours before serving.

Pavlova Ice Cream

Servings: 8

Ingredients

- 2 cups heavy cream
- 1 cup whole milk
- 3/4 cup granulated sugar
- 1 teaspoon pure vanilla extract

- 1 cup meringue pieces
- 1 cup fresh mixed berries (strawberries, blueberries, raspberries)

Instructions

In a medium bowl, whisk together the cream, milk, sugar, and vanilla extract until the sugar is completely dissolved.

Pour the mixture into the KitchenAid Ice Cream Attachment.

Churn on low speed for 25-30 minutes, or until the mixture reaches a soft-serve consistency.

In the last 5 minutes of churning, add the meringue pieces and mixed berries.

Transfer the ice cream to a lidded container and freeze for at least 2 hours before serving.

Speculoos Ice Cream

Servings: 8

Ingredients

- 2 cups heavy cream
- 1 cup whole milk
- 3/4 cup granulated sugar
- 1/2 cup speculoos cookie butter
- 1 teaspoon ground cinnamon
- 1 teaspoon pure vanilla extract
- 1 cup speculoos cookies, crumbled

Instructions

In a medium bowl, whisk together the cream, milk, sugar, cookie butter, cinnamon, and vanilla extract until the sugar is completely dissolved.

Pour the mixture into the KitchenAid Ice Cream Attachment.

Churn on low speed for 25-30 minutes, or until the mixture reaches a soft-serve consistency.

In the last 5 minutes of churning, add the crumbled speculoos cookies.

Transfer the ice cream to a lidded container and freeze for at least 2 hours before serving.

Ube Ice Cream

Servings: 8

Ingredients

- 2 cups heavy cream
- 1 cup whole milk
- 3/4 cup granulated sugar
- 1 cup ube (purple yam) jam
- 1 teaspoon pure vanilla extract

Instructions

In a medium bowl, whisk together the cream, milk, sugar, ube jam, and vanilla extract until the sugar is completely dissolved.

Pour the mixture into the KitchenAid Ice Cream Attachment.

Churn on low speed for 25-30 minutes, or until the mixture reaches a soft-serve consistency.

Transfer the ice cream to a lidded container and freeze for at least 2 hours before serving.

Black Forest Ice Cream

Servings: 8

Ingredients

- 2 cups heavy cream
- 1 cup whole milk
- 3/4 cup granulated sugar
- 1/2 cup unsweetened cocoa powder

- 1 teaspoon pure vanilla extract
- 1 cup cherry pie filling
- 1/2 cup chocolate chunks

Instructions

In a medium bowl, whisk together the cream, milk, sugar, cocoa powder, and vanilla extract until smooth and the sugar is dissolved.

Pour the mixture into the KitchenAid Ice Cream Attachment.

Churn on low speed for 25-30 minutes, or until the mixture reaches a soft-serve consistency.

In the last 5 minutes of churning, add the cherry pie filling and chocolate chunks.

Transfer the ice cream to a lidded container and freeze for at least 2 hours before serving.

Pineapple Coconut Ice Cream

Servings: 8

Ingredients

- 2 cups heavy cream
- 1 cup coconut milk
- 3/4 cup granulated sugar
- 1 teaspoon pure vanilla extract
- 1 cup fresh pineapple, diced

Instructions

In a medium bowl, whisk together the cream, coconut milk, sugar, and vanilla extract until the sugar is completely dissolved.

Pour the mixture into the KitchenAid Ice Cream Attachment.

Churn on low speed for 25-30 minutes, or until the mixture reaches a soft-serve consistency.

In the last 5 minutes of churning, add the diced pineapple.

Transfer the ice cream to a lidded container and freeze for at least 2 hours before serving.

Amarula Ice Cream

Servings: 8

Ingredients

- 2 cups heavy cream
- 1 cup whole milk
- 3/4 cup granulated sugar
- 1/2 cup Amarula liqueur
- 1 teaspoon pure vanilla extract

Instructions

In a medium bowl, whisk together the cream, milk, sugar, Amarula, and vanilla extract until the sugar is completely dissolved.

Pour the mixture into the KitchenAid Ice Cream Attachment.

Churn on low speed for 25-30 minutes, or until the mixture reaches a soft-serve consistency.

Transfer the ice cream to a lidded container and freeze for at least 2 hours before serving.

Orange Blossom Ice Cream

Servings: 8

Ingredients
- 2 cups heavy cream
- 1 cup whole milk
- 3/4 cup granulated sugar
- 2 tablespoons orange blossom water
- 1 teaspoon pure vanilla extract

Instructions

In a medium bowl, whisk together the cream, milk, sugar, orange blossom water, and vanilla extract until the sugar is completely dissolved.

Pour the mixture into the KitchenAid Ice Cream Attachment.

Churn on low speed for 25-30 minutes, or until the mixture reaches a soft-serve consistency.

Transfer the ice cream to a lidded container and freeze for at least 2 hours before serving.

Princess Cake Ice Cream

Servings: 8

Ingredients

- 2 cups heavy cream
- 1 cup whole milk
- 3/4 cup granulated sugar
- 1/2 cup marzipan, chopped
- 1 teaspoon pure vanilla extract
- 1/2 cup raspberry jam
- 1 cup sponge cake pieces

Instructions

In a medium bowl, whisk together the cream, milk, sugar, marzipan, and vanilla extract until the sugar is completely dissolved.

Pour the mixture into the KitchenAid Ice Cream Attachment.

Churn on low speed for 25-30 minutes, or until the mixture reaches a soft-serve consistency.

In the last 5 minutes of churning, add the raspberry jam and sponge cake pieces.

Transfer the ice cream to a lidded container and freeze for at least 2 hours before serving.

Olive Oil Ice Cream

Servings: 8

Ingredients

- 2 cups heavy cream
- 2 cups whole milk
- 3/4 cup granulated sugar
- 1/2 cup high-quality extra virgin olive oil
- 1 teaspoon pure vanilla extract
- Pinch of sea salt

Instructions

In a medium bowl, whisk together the heavy cream, whole milk, sugar, olive oil, vanilla extract, and sea salt until the sugar is completely dissolved.

Pour the mixture into the KitchenAid Ice Cream Attachment.

Churn on low speed for 20-25 minutes, or until the mixture reaches a soft-serve consistency.

Transfer the ice cream to a lidded container and freeze for at least 2 hours before serving.

Goat Cheese and Fig Ice Cream

Servings: 8

Ingredients

- 2 cups heavy cream
- 2 cups whole milk
- 3/4 cup granulated sugar
- 6 oz goat cheese, softened
- 1 teaspoon pure vanilla extract
- 1 cup chopped dried figs
- Pinch of salt

Instructions

In a medium bowl, whisk together the heavy cream, whole milk, sugar, goat cheese, vanilla extract, and salt until the sugar and goat cheese are completely dissolved and smooth.

Stir in the chopped figs.

Pour the mixture into the KitchenAid Ice Cream Attachment.

Churn on low speed for 20-25 minutes, or until the mixture reaches a soft-serve consistency.

Transfer the ice cream to a lidded container and freeze for at least 2 hours before serving.

Blue Cheese and Honey Ice Cream

Servings: 8

Ingredients

- 2 cups heavy cream
- 2 cups whole milk
- 3/4 cup granulated sugar
- 1/2 cup crumbled blue cheese
- 1/4 cup honey
- 1 teaspoon pure vanilla extract
- Pinch of salt

Instructions

In a medium bowl, whisk together the heavy cream, whole milk, sugar, blue cheese, honey, vanilla extract, and salt until the sugar is completely dissolved and smooth.

Pour the mixture into the KitchenAid Ice Cream Attachment.

Churn on low speed for 20-25 minutes, or until the mixture reaches a soft-serve consistency.

Transfer the ice cream to a lidded container and freeze for at least 2 hours before serving.

Brown Butter Ice Cream

Servings: 8

Ingredients

- 1 cup unsalted butter
- 2 cups heavy cream
- 2 cups whole milk
- 1 cup granulated sugar
- 1 teaspoon pure vanilla extract
- Pinch of salt

Instructions

In a saucepan, melt the butter over medium heat and cook until it turns golden brown and has a nutty aroma, about 5-7 minutes. Remove from heat and let cool slightly.

In a medium bowl, whisk together the browned butter, heavy cream, whole milk, sugar, vanilla extract, and salt until the sugar is completely dissolved.

Pour the mixture into the KitchenAid Ice Cream Attachment.

Churn on low speed for 20-25 minutes, or until the mixture reaches a soft-serve consistency.

Transfer the ice cream to a lidded container and freeze for at least 2 hours before serving.

Saffron Ice Cream

Servings: 8

Ingredients

- 2 cups heavy cream
- 2 cups whole milk
- 3/4 cup granulated sugar
- 1/4 teaspoon saffron threads
- 1 teaspoon pure vanilla extract

- Pinch of salt

Instructions

In a small bowl, soak the saffron threads in 2 tablespoons of warm milk for 10 minutes.

In a medium bowl, whisk together the heavy cream, whole milk, sugar, saffron mixture, vanilla extract, and salt until the sugar is completely dissolved.

Pour the mixture into the KitchenAid Ice Cream Attachment.

Churn on low speed for 20-25 minutes, or until the mixture reaches a soft-serve consistency.

Transfer the ice cream to a lidded container and freeze for at least 2 hours before serving.

Matcha Green Tea Ice Cream

Servings: 8

Ingredients

- 2 cups heavy cream
- 2 cups whole milk
- 3/4 cup granulated sugar
- 2 tablespoons matcha green tea powder
- 1 teaspoon pure vanilla extract
- Pinch of salt

Instructions

In a medium bowl, whisk together the heavy cream, whole milk, sugar, matcha powder, vanilla extract, and salt until the sugar and matcha powder are completely dissolved.

Pour the mixture into the KitchenAid Ice Cream Attachment.

Churn on low speed for 20-25 minutes, or until the mixture reaches a soft-serve consistency.

Transfer the ice cream to a lidded container and freeze for at least 2 hours before serving.

Avocado Lime Ice Cream

Servings: 8

Ingredients

- 3 ripe avocados, mashed
- 2 cups heavy cream
- 2 cups whole milk
- 3/4 cup granulated sugar
- 2 tablespoons lime juice
- 1 teaspoon lime zest
- 1 teaspoon pure vanilla extract
- Pinch of salt

Instructions

In a medium bowl, whisk together the mashed avocados, heavy cream, whole milk, sugar, lime juice, lime zest, vanilla extract, and salt until the sugar is completely dissolved.

Pour the mixture into the KitchenAid Ice Cream Attachment.

Churn on low speed for 20-25 minutes, or until the mixture reaches a soft-serve consistency.

Transfer the ice cream to a lidded container and freeze for at least 2 hours before serving.

Chai Spice Ice Cream

Servings: 8

Ingredients

- 2 cups heavy cream
- 2 cups whole milk
- 1 cup granulated sugar
- 3 chai tea bags
- 1 teaspoon ground cinnamon

- 1/2 teaspoon ground ginger
- 1/4 teaspoon ground cardamom
- 1/4 teaspoon ground cloves
- 1 teaspoon pure vanilla extract
- Pinch of salt

Instructions

In a saucepan, combine the heavy cream and whole milk. Heat over medium heat until the mixture is hot but not boiling.

Remove from heat, add the chai tea bags, and let steep for 10 minutes. Remove the tea bags, squeezing out any excess liquid.

Whisk in the sugar, spices, vanilla extract, and salt until the sugar is completely dissolved.

Chill the mixture in the refrigerator until completely cool.

Pour the mixture into the KitchenAid Ice Cream Attachment.

Churn on low speed for 20-25 minutes, or until the mixture reaches a soft-serve consistency.

Transfer the ice cream to a lidded container and freeze for at least 2 hours before serving.

Sweet Corn Ice Cream

Servings: 8

Ingredients

- 2 cups heavy cream
- 2 cups whole milk
- 1 cup granulated sugar
- 2 cups fresh or frozen corn kernels
- 1 teaspoon pure vanilla extract
- Pinch of salt

Instructions

In a blender or food processor, puree the corn kernels until smooth.

In a medium bowl, whisk together the corn puree, heavy cream, whole milk, sugar, vanilla extract, and salt until the sugar is completely dissolved.

Pour the mixture into the KitchenAid Ice Cream Attachment.

Churn on low speed for 20-25 minutes, or until the mixture reaches a soft-serve consistency.

Transfer the ice cream to a lidded container and freeze for at least 2 hours before serving.

Roasted Strawberry Balsamic Ice Cream

Servings: 8

Ingredients

- 2 cups fresh strawberries, hulled and halved
- 2 tablespoons balsamic vinegar
- 2 cups heavy cream
- 2 cups whole milk
- 3/4 cup granulated sugar
- 1 teaspoon pure vanilla extract
- Pinch of salt

Instructions

Preheat the oven to 375°F (190°C). Toss the strawberries with the balsamic vinegar and spread them on a baking sheet. Roast for 20-25 minutes, or until the strawberries are soft and caramelized. Let cool.

In a blender or food processor, puree the roasted strawberries until smooth.

In a medium bowl, whisk together the strawberry puree, heavy cream, whole milk, sugar, vanilla extract, and salt until the sugar is completely dissolved.

Pour the mixture into the KitchenAid Ice Cream Attachment.

Churn on low speed for 20-25 minutes, or until the mixture reaches a soft-serve consistency.

Transfer the ice cream to a lidded container and freeze for at least 2 hours before serving.

Spiced Pumpkin Ice Cream

Servings: 8

Ingredients

- 2 cups heavy cream
- 2 cups whole milk
- 3/4 cup granulated sugar
- 1 cup pumpkin puree
- 1 teaspoon ground cinnamon
- 1/2 teaspoon ground ginger
- 1/4 teaspoon ground nutmeg
- 1/4 teaspoon ground cloves
- 1 teaspoon pure vanilla extract
- Pinch of salt

Instructions

In a medium bowl, whisk together the heavy cream, whole milk, sugar, pumpkin puree, spices, vanilla extract, and salt until the sugar is completely dissolved.

Pour the mixture into the KitchenAid Ice Cream Attachment.

Churn on low speed for 20-25 minutes, or until the mixture reaches a soft-serve consistency.

Transfer the ice cream to a lidded container and freeze for at least 2 hours before serving.

Thai Tea Ice Cream

Servings: 8

Ingredients

- 2 cups heavy cream
- 2 cups whole milk
- 1 cup granulated sugar
- 4 Thai tea bags
- 1 teaspoon pure vanilla extract
- Pinch of salt

Instructions

In a saucepan, combine the heavy cream and whole milk. Heat over medium heat until the mixture is hot but not boiling.

Remove from heat, add the Thai tea bags, and let steep for 10 minutes. Remove the tea bags, squeezing out any excess liquid.

Whisk in the sugar, vanilla extract, and salt until the sugar is completely dissolved.

Chill the mixture in the refrigerator until completely cool.

Pour the mixture into the KitchenAid Ice Cream Attachment.

Churn on low speed for 20-25 minutes, or until the mixture reaches a soft-serve consistency.

Transfer the ice cream to a lidded container and freeze for at least 2 hours before serving.

Gingerbread Ice Cream

Servings: 8

Ingredients

- 2 cups heavy cream
- 2 cups whole milk

- 3/4 cup granulated sugar
- 1/2 cup molasses
- 1 teaspoon ground ginger
- 1 teaspoon ground cinnamon
- 1/2 teaspoon ground cloves
- 1/4 teaspoon ground nutmeg
- 1 teaspoon pure vanilla extract
- Pinch of salt

Instructions

In a medium bowl, whisk together the heavy cream, whole milk, sugar, molasses, spices, vanilla extract, and salt until the sugar is completely dissolved.

Pour the mixture into the KitchenAid Ice Cream Attachment.

Churn on low speed for 20-25 minutes, or until the mixture reaches a soft-serve consistency.

Transfer the ice cream to a lidded container and freeze for at least 2 hours before serving.

Basil Ice Cream

Servings: 8

Ingredients

- 2 cups heavy cream
- 2 cups whole milk
- 3/4 cup granulated sugar
- 1 cup fresh basil leaves, finely chopped
- 1 teaspoon pure vanilla extract
- Pinch of salt

Instructions

In a medium bowl, whisk together the heavy cream, whole milk, sugar, basil leaves, vanilla

extract, and salt until the sugar is completely dissolved.

Pour the mixture into the KitchenAid Ice Cream Attachment.

Churn on low speed for 20-25 minutes, or until the mixture reaches a soft-serve consistency.

Transfer the ice cream to a lidded container and freeze for at least 2 hours before serving.

Lemon Basil Ice Cream

Servings: 8

Ingredients

- 2 cups heavy cream
- 2 cups whole milk
- 3/4 cup granulated sugar
- 1/4 cup fresh lemon juice
- 1 tablespoon lemon zest
- 1/2 cup fresh basil leaves, finely chopped
- 1 teaspoon pure vanilla extract
- Pinch of salt

Instructions

In a medium bowl, whisk together the heavy cream, whole milk, sugar, lemon juice, lemon zest, basil leaves, vanilla extract, and salt until the sugar is completely dissolved.

Pour the mixture into the KitchenAid Ice Cream Attachment.

Churn on low speed for 20-25 minutes, or until the mixture reaches a soft-serve consistency.

Transfer the ice cream to a lidded container and freeze for at least 2 hours before serving.

4. Dairy-Free and Vegan Options

Blueberry Lemon Sorbet

Servings: 8

Ingredients

- 4 cups fresh blueberries
- 1/2 cup granulated sugar
- 1/4 cup water
- 2 tablespoons fresh lemon juice
- 1 tablespoon lemon zest

Instructions

In a blender or food processor, puree the blueberries until smooth. Strain through a fine-mesh sieve to remove the skins.

In a medium bowl, whisk together the blueberry puree, sugar, water, lemon juice, and lemon zest until the sugar is completely dissolved.

Pour the mixture into the KitchenAid Ice Cream Attachment.

Churn on low speed for 20-25 minutes, or until the mixture reaches a sorbet-like consistency.

Transfer the sorbet to a lidded container and freeze for at least 2 hours before serving.

Chai Spice Ice Cream

Servings: 8

Ingredients

- 2 cans (14 oz each) full-fat coconut milk
- 3/4 cup granulated sugar
- 2 tablespoons loose-leaf chai tea or 4 chai tea bags
- 1 teaspoon pure vanilla extract
- Pinch of salt

Instructions

In a saucepan, heat the coconut milk until it just begins to simmer. Remove from heat and add the chai tea. Let steep for 10 minutes, then strain.

In a medium bowl, whisk together the infused coconut milk, sugar, vanilla extract, and salt until the sugar is completely dissolved.

Pour the mixture into the KitchenAid Ice Cream Attachment.

Churn on low speed for 25-30 minutes, or until the mixture reaches a soft-serve consistency.

Transfer the ice cream to a lidded container and freeze for at least 2 hours before serving.

Coconut Vanilla Bean Ice Cream

Servings: 8

Ingredients

- 2 cans (14 oz each) full-fat coconut milk
- 3/4 cup granulated sugar
- 1 vanilla bean, split and seeds scraped
- 1 teaspoon pure vanilla extract
- Pinch of salt

Instructions

In a medium bowl, whisk together the coconut milk, sugar, vanilla bean seeds, vanilla extract, and salt until the sugar is completely dissolved.

Pour the mixture into the KitchenAid Ice Cream Attachment.

Churn on low speed for 25-30 minutes, or until the mixture reaches a soft-serve consistency.

Transfer the ice cream to a lidded container and freeze for at least 2 hours before serving.

Vegan Pistachio Ice Cream

Servings: 8

Ingredients

- 2 cans (14 oz each) full-fat coconut milk
- 3/4 cup granulated sugar
- 1 cup unsalted shelled pistachios
- 1 teaspoon pure vanilla extract
- Pinch of salt

Instructions

In a food processor, finely grind the pistachios.

In a medium bowl, whisk together the coconut milk, sugar, ground pistachios, vanilla extract, and salt until the sugar is completely dissolved.

Pour the mixture into the KitchenAid Ice Cream Attachment.

Churn on low speed for 25-30 minutes, or until the mixture reaches a soft-serve consistency.

Transfer the ice cream to a lidded container and freeze for at least 2 hours before serving.

Chocolate Almond Milk Ice Cream

Servings: 8

Ingredients

- 3 cups almond milk
- 1 cup coconut cream
- 3/4 cup granulated sugar
- 1/2 cup unsweetened cocoa powder
- 1 teaspoon pure vanilla extract
- Pinch of salt

Instructions

In a medium bowl, whisk together the almond milk, coconut cream, sugar, cocoa powder, vanilla extract, and salt until the sugar and cocoa are completely dissolved.

Pour the mixture into the KitchenAid Ice Cream Attachment.

Churn on low speed for 25-30 minutes, or until the mixture reaches a soft-serve consistency.

Transfer the ice cream to a lidded container and freeze for at least 2 hours before serving.

Mango Sorbet

Servings: 8

Ingredients

- 4 cups fresh mango, peeled and diced
- 1/2 cup granulated sugar
- 1/4 cup water
- 2 tablespoons fresh lime juice

Instructions

In a blender or food processor, puree the mango until smooth.

In a medium bowl, whisk together the mango puree, sugar, water, and lime juice until the sugar is completely dissolved.

Pour the mixture into the KitchenAid Ice Cream Attachment.

Churn on low speed for 20-25 minutes, or until the mixture reaches a sorbet-like consistency.

Transfer the sorbet to a lidded container and freeze for at least 2 hours before serving.

Strawberry Coconut Milk Ice Cream

Servings: 8

Ingredients

- 2 cans (14 oz each) full-fat coconut milk
- 1 cup fresh strawberries, hulled and sliced
- 3/4 cup granulated sugar
- 1 teaspoon pure vanilla extract
- Pinch of salt

Instructions

In a blender or food processor, puree the strawberries until smooth.

In a medium bowl, whisk together the coconut milk, strawberry puree, sugar, vanilla extract, and salt until the sugar is completely dissolved.

Pour the mixture into the KitchenAid Ice Cream Attachment.

Churn on low speed for 25-30 minutes, or until the mixture reaches a soft-serve consistency.

Transfer the ice cream to a lidded container and freeze for at least 2 hours before serving.

Avocado Lime Ice Cream

Servings: 8

Ingredients

- 3 ripe avocados, peeled and pitted
- 1 can (14 oz) full-fat coconut milk
- 3/4 cup granulated sugar
- 1/4 cup fresh lime juice
- 1 tablespoon lime zest
- Pinch of salt

Instructions

In a blender or food processor, puree the avocados until smooth.

In a medium bowl, whisk together the avocado puree, coconut milk, sugar, lime juice, lime zest, and salt until the sugar is completely dissolved.

Pour the mixture into the KitchenAid Ice Cream Attachment.

Churn on low speed for 25-30 minutes, or until the mixture reaches a soft-serve consistency.

Transfer the ice cream to a lidded container and freeze for at least 2 hours before serving.

Pineapple Coconut Sorbet

Servings: 8

Ingredients

- 4 cups fresh pineapple, peeled and diced
- 1/2 cup coconut water
- 1/2 cup granulated sugar
- 1 tablespoon fresh lime juice

Instructions

In a blender or food processor, puree the pineapple until smooth.

In a medium bowl, whisk together the pineapple puree, coconut water, sugar, and lime juice until the sugar is completely dissolved.

Pour the mixture into the KitchenAid Ice Cream Attachment.

Churn on low speed for 20-25 minutes, or until the mixture reaches a sorbet-like consistency.

Transfer the sorbet to a lidded container and freeze for at least 2 hours before serving.

Matcha Green Tea Coconut Milk Ice Cream

Servings: 8

Ingredients

- 2 cans (14 oz each) full-fat coconut milk
- 3/4 cup granulated sugar
- 2 tablespoons matcha green tea powder
- 1 teaspoon pure vanilla extract
- Pinch of salt

Instructions

In a medium bowl, whisk together the coconut milk, sugar, matcha powder, vanilla extract, and salt until the sugar and matcha are completely dissolved.

Pour the mixture into the KitchenAid Ice Cream Attachment.

Churn on low speed for 25-30 minutes, or until the mixture reaches a soft-serve consistency.

Transfer the ice cream to a lidded container and freeze for at least 2 hours before serving.

Raspberry Sorbet

Servings: 8

Ingredients

- 4 cups fresh raspberries
- 1/2 cup granulated sugar
- 1/4 cup water
- 1 tablespoon fresh lemon juice

Instructions

In a blender or food processor, puree the raspberries until smooth. Strain through a fine-mesh sieve to remove the seeds.

In a medium bowl, whisk together the raspberry puree, sugar, water, and lemon juice until the sugar is completely dissolved.

Pour the mixture into the KitchenAid Ice Cream Attachment.

Churn on low speed for 20-25 minutes, or until the mixture reaches a sorbet-like consistency.

Transfer the sorbet to a lidded container and freeze for at least 2 hours before serving.

Banana Peanut Butter Ice Cream

Servings: 8

Ingredients

- 4 ripe bananas, peeled and sliced
- 1 can (14 oz) full-fat coconut milk
- 3/4 cup creamy peanut butter
- 1/2 cup granulated sugar
- 1 teaspoon pure vanilla extract
- Pinch of salt

Instructions

In a blender or food processor, puree the bananas until smooth.

In a medium bowl, whisk together the banana puree, coconut milk, peanut butter, sugar, vanilla extract, and salt until the sugar is completely dissolved.

Pour the mixture into the KitchenAid Ice Cream Attachment.

Churn on low speed for 25-30 minutes, or until the mixture reaches a soft-serve consistency.

Transfer the ice cream to a lidded container and freeze for at least 2 hours before serving.

Lemon Basil Sorbet

Servings: 8

Ingredients

- 4 cups water
- 1 cup granulated sugar
- 1 cup fresh lemon juice
- 1/4 cup fresh basil leaves, chopped
- 1 tablespoon lemon zest

Instructions

In a saucepan, combine the water and sugar. Bring to a boil, stirring until the sugar is dissolved. Remove from heat and let cool.

In a medium bowl, whisk together the cooled syrup, lemon juice, basil, and lemon zest.

Pour the mixture into the KitchenAid Ice Cream Attachment.

Churn on low speed for 20-25 minutes, or until the mixture reaches a sorbet-like consistency.

Transfer the sorbet to a lidded container and freeze for at least 2 hours before serving.

Espresso Chocolate Chip Ice Cream

Servings: 8

Ingredients

- 2 cans (14 oz each) full-fat coconut milk
- 3/4 cup granulated sugar
- 1/4 cup espresso or strong coffee, cooled
- 1 teaspoon pure vanilla extract
- 1 cup dairy-free chocolate chips
- Pinch of salt

Instructions

In a medium bowl, whisk together the coconut milk, sugar, espresso, vanilla extract, and salt until the sugar is completely dissolved.

Stir in the chocolate chips.

Pour the mixture into the KitchenAid Ice Cream Attachment.

Churn on low speed for 25-30 minutes, or until the mixture reaches a soft-serve consistency.

Transfer the ice cream to a lidded container and freeze for at least 2 hours before serving.

Pumpkin Spice Ice Cream

Servings: 8

Ingredients

- 2 cans (14 oz each) full-fat coconut milk
- 1 cup pumpkin puree
- 3/4 cup granulated sugar
- 1 teaspoon ground cinnamon
- 1/2 teaspoon ground ginger
- 1/4 teaspoon ground nutmeg
- 1 teaspoon pure vanilla extract
- Pinch of salt

Instructions

In a medium bowl, whisk together the coconut milk, pumpkin puree, sugar, spices, vanilla extract, and salt until the sugar is completely dissolved.

Pour the mixture into the KitchenAid Ice Cream Attachment.

Churn on low speed for 25-30 minutes, or until the mixture reaches a soft-serve consistency.

Transfer the ice cream to a lidded container and freeze for at least 2 hours before serving.

Blackberry Coconut Milk Ice Cream

Servings: 8

Ingredients

- 2 cans (14 oz each) full-fat coconut milk
- 1 cup fresh blackberries
- 3/4 cup granulated sugar
- 1 teaspoon pure vanilla extract
- Pinch of salt

Instructions

In a blender or food processor, puree the blackberries until smooth. Strain through a fine-mesh sieve to remove the seeds.

In a medium bowl, whisk together the coconut milk, blackberry puree, sugar, vanilla extract, and salt until the sugar is completely dissolved.

Pour the mixture into the KitchenAid Ice Cream Attachment.

Churn on low speed for 25-30 minutes, or until the mixture reaches a soft-serve consistency.

Transfer the ice cream to a lidded container and freeze for at least 2 hours before serving.

Spiced Apple Sorbet

Servings: 8

Ingredients

- 4 cups apple cider
- 1/2 cup granulated sugar
- 1/4 cup fresh lemon juice
- 1 teaspoon ground cinnamon
- 1/2 teaspoon ground nutmeg
- 1/4 teaspoon ground cloves

Instructions

In a medium bowl, whisk together the apple cider, sugar, lemon juice, and spices until the sugar is completely dissolved.

Pour the mixture into the KitchenAid Ice Cream Attachment.

Churn on low speed for 20-25 minutes, or until the mixture reaches a sorbet-like consistency.

Transfer the sorbet to a lidded container and freeze for at least 2 hours before serving.

Mocha Almond Fudge Ice Cream

Servings: 8

Ingredients

- 2 cans (14 oz each) full-fat coconut milk
- 3/4 cup granulated sugar
- 1/4 cup espresso or strong coffee, cooled
- 1/4 cup cocoa powder
- 1 teaspoon pure vanilla extract
- 1/2 cup chopped toasted almonds
- 1/2 cup dairy-free fudge sauce
- Pinch of salt

Instructions

In a medium bowl, whisk together the coconut milk, sugar, espresso, cocoa powder, vanilla extract, and salt until the sugar and cocoa are completely dissolved.

Stir in the chopped almonds.

Pour the mixture into the KitchenAid Ice Cream Attachment.

Churn on low speed for 25-30 minutes, or until the mixture reaches a soft-serve consistency.

During the last 5 minutes of churning, slowly drizzle in the fudge sauce.

Transfer the ice cream to a lidded container and freeze for at least 2 hours before serving.

Dragon Fruit Sorbet

Servings: 8

Ingredients

- 4 cups dragon fruit, peeled and diced
- 1/2 cup granulated sugar
- 1/4 cup water
- 1 tablespoon fresh lemon juice

Instructions

In a blender or food processor, puree the dragon fruit until smooth.

In a medium bowl, whisk together the dragon fruit puree, sugar, water, and lemon juice until the sugar is completely dissolved.

Pour the mixture into the KitchenAid Ice Cream Attachment.

Churn on low speed for 20-25 minutes, or until the mixture reaches a sorbet-like consistency.

Transfer the sorbet to a lidded container and freeze for at least 2 hours before serving.

Honeydew Mint Sorbet

Servings: 8

Ingredients

- 4 cups honeydew melon, peeled and diced
- 1/2 cup granulated sugar
- 1/4 cup fresh mint leaves, chopped
- 2 tablespoons fresh lime juice

Instructions

In a blender or food processor, puree the honeydew melon until smooth.

In a medium bowl, whisk together the honeydew puree, sugar, mint, and lime juice until the sugar is completely dissolved.

Pour the mixture into the KitchenAid Ice Cream Attachment.

Churn on low speed for 20-25 minutes, or until the mixture reaches a sorbet-like consistency.

Transfer the sorbet to a lidded container and freeze for at least 2 hours before serving.

5. Sorbets and Gelatos

Lemon Sorbet

Servings: 8

Ingredients

- 4 cups water
- 1 cup granulated sugar
- 1 cup fresh lemon juice
- 1 tablespoon lemon zest

Instructions

In a saucepan, combine the water and sugar. Bring to a boil, stirring until the sugar is dissolved. Remove from heat and let cool.

In a medium bowl, whisk together the cooled syrup, lemon juice, and lemon zest.

Pour the mixture into the KitchenAid Ice Cream Attachment.

Churn on low speed for 20-25 minutes, or until the mixture reaches a sorbet-like consistency.

Transfer the sorbet to a lidded container and freeze for at least 2 hours before serving.

Cantaloupe Sorbet

Servings: 8

Ingredients

- 4 cups cantaloupe, peeled and diced
- 1/2 cup granulated sugar
- 1/4 cup water
- 1 tablespoon fresh lime juice

Instructions

In a blender or food processor, puree the cantaloupe until smooth.

In a medium bowl, whisk together the cantaloupe puree, sugar, water, and lime juice until the sugar is completely dissolved.

Pour the mixture into the KitchenAid Ice Cream Attachment.

Churn on low speed for 20-25 minutes, or until the mixture reaches a sorbet-like consistency.

Transfer the sorbet to a lidded container and freeze for at least 2 hours before serving.

Watermelon Mint Sorbet

Servings: 8

Ingredients

4 cups watermelon, seeded and diced

1/2 cup granulated sugar

1/4 cup water

1/4 cup fresh mint leaves, chopped

1 tablespoon fresh lime juice

Instructions

In a blender or food processor, puree the watermelon until smooth.

In a medium bowl, whisk together the watermelon puree, sugar, water, mint, and lime juice until the sugar is completely dissolved.

Pour the mixture into the KitchenAid Ice Cream Attachment.

Churn on low speed for 20-25 minutes, or until the mixture reaches a sorbet-like consistency.

Transfer the sorbet to a lidded container and freeze for at least 2 hours before serving.

Peach Sorbet

Servings: 8

Ingredients

- 4 cups fresh peaches, peeled and diced
- 1/2 cup granulated sugar
- 1/4 cup water
- 1 tablespoon fresh lemon juice

Instructions

In a blender or food processor, puree the peaches until smooth.

In a medium bowl, whisk together the peach puree, sugar, water, and lemon juice until the sugar is completely dissolved.

Pour the mixture into the KitchenAid Ice Cream Attachment.

Churn on low speed for 20-25 minutes, or until the mixture reaches a sorbet-like consistency.

Transfer the sorbet to a lidded container and freeze for at least 2 hours before serving.

Strawberry Basil Sorbet

Servings: 8

Ingredients

- 4 cups fresh strawberries, hulled
- 1/2 cup granulated sugar
- 1/4 cup water
- 1/4 cup fresh basil leaves, chopped
- 1 tablespoon fresh lemon juice

Instructions

In a blender or food processor, puree the strawberries until smooth.

In a medium bowl, whisk together the strawberry puree, sugar, water, basil, and lemon juice until the sugar is completely dissolved.

Pour the mixture into the KitchenAid Ice Cream Attachment.

Churn on low speed for 20-25 minutes, or until the mixture reaches a sorbet-like consistency.

Transfer the sorbet to a lidded container and freeze for at least 2 hours before serving.

Blood Orange Sorbet

Servings: 8

Ingredients

- 4 cups fresh blood orange juice
- 1/2 cup granulated sugar
- 1/4 cup water
- 1 tablespoon orange zest

Instructions

In a medium bowl, whisk together the blood orange juice, sugar, water, and orange zest until the sugar is completely dissolved.

Pour the mixture into the KitchenAid Ice Cream Attachment.

Churn on low speed for 20-25 minutes, or until the mixture reaches a sorbet-like consistency.

Transfer the sorbet to a lidded container and freeze for at least 2 hours before serving.

Pineapple Ginger Sorbet

Servings: 8

Ingredients

- 4 cups fresh pineapple, peeled and diced
- 1/2 cup granulated sugar
- 1/4 cup water
- 1 tablespoon fresh ginger, grated
- 1 tablespoon fresh lime juice

Instructions

In a blender or food processor, puree the pineapple until smooth.

In a medium bowl, whisk together the pineapple puree, sugar, water, ginger, and lime juice until the sugar is completely dissolved.

Pour the mixture into the KitchenAid Ice Cream Attachment.

Churn on low speed for 20-25 minutes, or until the mixture reaches a sorbet-like consistency.

Transfer the sorbet to a lidded container and freeze for at least 2 hours before serving.

Mango Gelato

Servings: 8

Ingredients

- 3 cups fresh mango, peeled and diced
- 1/2 cup granulated sugar
- 1 cup almond milk
- 1 teaspoon pure vanilla extract
- Pinch of salt

Instructions

In a blender or food processor, puree the mango until smooth.

In a medium bowl, whisk together the mango puree, sugar, almond milk, vanilla extract, and salt until the sugar is completely dissolved.

Pour the mixture into the KitchenAid Ice Cream Attachment.

Churn on low speed for 25-30 minutes, or until the mixture reaches a gelato-like consistency.

Transfer the gelato to a lidded container and freeze for at least 2 hours before serving.

Chocolate Hazelnut Gelato

Servings: 8

Ingredients

- 2 cups hazelnut milk
- 1 cup coconut cream
- 3/4 cup granulated sugar
- 1/2 cup unsweetened cocoa powder
- 1 teaspoon pure vanilla extract
- Pinch of salt

Instructions

In a medium bowl, whisk together the hazelnut milk, coconut cream, sugar, cocoa powder, vanilla extract, and salt until the sugar and cocoa are completely dissolved.

Pour the mixture into the KitchenAid Ice Cream Attachment.

Churn on low speed for 25-30 minutes, or until the mixture reaches a gelato-like consistency.

Transfer the gelato to a lidded container and freeze for at least 2 hours before serving.

Pistachio Gelato

Servings: 8

Ingredients

- 2 cups unsweetened almond milk
- 1 cup coconut cream
- 3/4 cup granulated sugar
- 1 cup unsalted shelled pistachios, finely ground
- 1 teaspoon pure vanilla extract
- Pinch of salt

Instructions

In a medium bowl, whisk together the almond milk, coconut cream, sugar, ground pistachios, vanilla extract, and salt until the sugar is completely dissolved.

Pour the mixture into the KitchenAid Ice Cream Attachment.

Churn on low speed for 25-30 minutes, or until the mixture reaches a gelato-like consistency.

Transfer the gelato to a lidded container and freeze for at least 2 hours before serving.

Espresso Gelato

Servings: 8

Ingredients

- 2 cups cashew milk
- 1 cup coconut cream
- 3/4 cup granulated sugar
- 1/4 cup espresso or strong coffee, cooled
- 1 teaspoon pure vanilla extract
- Pinch of salt

Instructions

In a medium bowl, whisk together the cashew milk, coconut cream, sugar, espresso, vanilla extract, and salt until the sugar is completely dissolved.

Pour the mixture into the KitchenAid Ice Cream Attachment.

Churn on low speed for 25-30 minutes, or until the mixture reaches a gelato-like consistency.

Transfer the gelato to a lidded container and freeze for at least 2 hours before serving.

Raspberry Lemon Sorbet

Servings: 8

Ingredients

- 4 cups fresh raspberries
- 1/2 cup granulated sugar
- 1/4 cup water
- 1/4 cup fresh lemon juice
- 1 tablespoon lemon zest

Instructions

In a blender or food processor, puree the raspberries until smooth. Strain through a fine-mesh sieve to remove the seeds.

In a medium bowl, whisk together the raspberry puree, sugar, water, lemon juice, and lemon zest until the sugar is completely dissolved.

Pour the mixture into the KitchenAid Ice Cream Attachment.

Churn on low speed for 20-25 minutes, or until the mixture reaches a sorbet-like consistency.

Transfer the sorbet to a lidded container and freeze for at least 2 hours before serving.

Kiwi Sorbet

Servings: 8

Ingredients

- 4 cups kiwi, peeled and diced
- 1/2 cup granulated sugar
- 1/4 cup water
- 1 tablespoon fresh lemon juice

Instructions

In a blender or food processor, puree the kiwi until smooth.

In a medium bowl, whisk together the kiwi puree, sugar, water, and lemon juice until the sugar is completely dissolved.

Pour the mixture into the KitchenAid Ice Cream Attachment.

Churn on low speed for 20-25 minutes, or until the mixture reaches a sorbet-like consistency.

Transfer the sorbet to a lidded container and freeze for at least 2 hours before serving.

Pomegranate Sorbet

Servings: 8

Ingredients

- 4 cups pomegranate juice
- 1/2 cup granulated sugar
- 1/4 cup water
- 1 tablespoon fresh lemon juice

Instructions

In a medium bowl, whisk together the pomegranate juice, sugar, water, and lemon juice until the sugar is completely dissolved.

Pour the mixture into the KitchenAid Ice Cream Attachment.

Churn on low speed for 20-25 minutes, or until the mixture reaches a sorbet-like consistency.

Transfer the sorbet to a lidded container and freeze for at least 2 hours before serving.

Chocolate Gelato

Servings: 8

Ingredients

- 2 cups almond milk
- 1 cup coconut cream
- 3/4 cup granulated sugar
- 1/2 cup unsweetened cocoa powder
- 1 teaspoon pure vanilla extract
- Pinch of salt

Instructions

In a medium bowl, whisk together the almond milk, coconut cream, sugar, cocoa powder, vanilla extract, and salt until the sugar and cocoa are completely dissolved.

Pour the mixture into the KitchenAid Ice Cream Attachment.

Churn on low speed for 25-30 minutes, or until the mixture reaches a gelato-like consistency.

Transfer the gelato to a lidded container and freeze for at least 2 hours before serving.

Coconut Gelato

Servings: 8

Ingredients

- 2 cans (14 oz each) full-fat coconut milk
- 3/4 cup granulated sugar
- 1 teaspoon pure vanilla extract
- Pinch of salt

Instructions

In a medium bowl, whisk together the coconut milk, sugar, vanilla extract, and salt until the sugar is completely dissolved.

Pour the mixture into the KitchenAid Ice Cream Attachment.

Churn on low speed for 25-30 minutes, or until the mixture reaches a gelato-like consistency.

Transfer the gelato to a lidded container and freeze for at least 2 hours before serving.

Blueberry Sorbet

Servings: 8

Ingredients

- 4 cups fresh blueberries
- 1/2 cup granulated sugar
- 1/4 cup water

- 1 tablespoon fresh lemon juice

Instructions

In a blender or food processor, puree the blueberries until smooth. Strain through a fine-mesh sieve to remove the skins.

In a medium bowl, whisk together the blueberry puree, sugar, water, and lemon juice until the sugar is completely dissolved.

Pour the mixture into the KitchenAid Ice Cream Attachment.

Churn on low speed for 20-25 minutes, or until the mixture reaches a sorbet-like consistency.

Transfer the sorbet to a lidded container and freeze for at least 2 hours before serving.

Matcha Green Tea Gelato

Servings: 8

Ingredients

- 2 cups cashew milk
- 1 cup coconut cream
- 3/4 cup granulated sugar
- 2 tablespoons matcha green tea powder
- 1 teaspoon pure vanilla extract
- Pinch of salt

Instructions

In a medium bowl, whisk together the cashew milk, coconut cream, sugar, matcha powder, vanilla extract, and salt until the sugar and matcha are completely dissolved.

Pour the mixture into the KitchenAid Ice Cream Attachment.

Churn on low speed for 25-30 minutes, or until the mixture reaches a gelato-like consistency.

Transfer the gelato to a lidded container and freeze for at least 2 hours before serving.

Apricot Sorbet

Servings: 8

Ingredients

- 4 cups fresh apricots, pitted and diced
- 1/2 cup granulated sugar
- 1/4 cup water
- 1 tablespoon fresh lemon juice

Instructions

In a blender or food processor, puree the apricots until smooth.

In a medium bowl, whisk together the apricot puree, sugar, water, and lemon juice until the sugar is completely dissolved.

Pour the mixture into the KitchenAid Ice Cream Attachment.

Churn on low speed for 20-25 minutes, or until the mixture reaches a sorbet-like consistency.

Transfer the sorbet to a lidded container and freeze for at least 2 hours before serving.

Black Cherry Gelato

Servings: 8

Ingredients

- 3 cups fresh black cherries, pitted and halved
- 1/2 cup granulated sugar
- 1 cup almond milk
- 1 teaspoon pure vanilla extract
- Pinch of salt

Instructions

In a blender or food processor, puree the cherries until smooth.

In a medium bowl, whisk together the cherry puree, sugar, almond milk, vanilla extract, and salt until the sugar is completely dissolved.

Pour the mixture into the KitchenAid Ice Cream Attachment.

Churn on low speed for 25-30 minutes, or until the mixture reaches a gelato-like consistency.

Transfer the gelato to a lidded container and freeze for at least 2 hours before serving.

6. Alcohol-Infused Ice Creams

Rum Raisin Ice Cream

Servings: 8

Ingredients

- 2 cups heavy cream
- 1 cup whole milk
- 3/4 cup granulated sugar
- 1 teaspoon pure vanilla extract
- 1/2 cup dark rum
- 1 cup raisins

Instructions

In a small bowl, soak the raisins in the dark rum for at least 2 hours or overnight.

In a medium bowl, whisk together the cream, milk, sugar, and vanilla extract until the sugar is completely dissolved.

Stir in the rum-soaked raisins and any remaining rum.

Pour the mixture into the KitchenAid Ice Cream Attachment.

Churn on low speed for 25-30 minutes, or until the mixture reaches a soft-serve consistency.

Transfer the ice cream to a lidded container and freeze for at least 2 hours before serving.

Piña Colada Ice Cream

Servings: 8

Ingredients

- 2 cups coconut milk
- 1 cup heavy cream
- 3/4 cup granulated sugar
- 1 cup crushed pineapple, drained
- 1/2 cup coconut rum
- 1 teaspoon pure vanilla extract

Instructions

In a medium bowl, whisk together the coconut milk, cream, sugar, pineapple, rum, and vanilla extract until the sugar is completely dissolved.

Pour the mixture into the KitchenAid Ice Cream Attachment.

Churn on low speed for 25-30 minutes, or until the mixture reaches a soft-serve consistency.

Transfer the ice cream to a lidded container and freeze for at least 2 hours before serving.

Bourbon Vanilla Ice Cream

Servings: 8

Ingredients

- 2 cups heavy cream
- 1 cup whole milk
- 3/4 cup granulated sugar
- 2 tablespoons bourbon
- 1 teaspoon pure vanilla extract

Instructions

In a medium bowl, whisk together the cream, milk, sugar, bourbon, and vanilla extract until the sugar is completely dissolved.

Pour the mixture into the KitchenAid Ice Cream Attachment.

Churn on low speed for 25-30 minutes, or until the mixture reaches a soft-serve consistency.

Transfer the ice cream to a lidded container and freeze for at least 2 hours before serving.

Irish Coffee Ice Cream

Servings: 8

Ingredients

- 2 cups heavy cream
- 1 cup whole milk
- 3/4 cup granulated sugar
- 1/4 cup strong brewed coffee, cooled
- 1/4 cup Irish whiskey
- 1 teaspoon pure vanilla extract

Instructions

In a medium bowl, whisk together the cream, milk, sugar, coffee, whiskey, and vanilla extract until the sugar is completely dissolved.

Pour the mixture into the KitchenAid Ice Cream Attachment.

Churn on low speed for 25-30 minutes, or until the mixture reaches a soft-serve consistency.

Transfer the ice cream to a lidded container and freeze for at least 2 hours before serving.

Margarita Sorbet

Servings: 8

Ingredients

- 4 cups water
- 1 cup granulated sugar
- 1 cup fresh lime juice
- 1/2 cup tequila
- 1/4 cup orange liqueur (such as Cointreau)
- 1 tablespoon lime zest

Instructions

In a saucepan, combine the water and sugar. Bring to a boil, stirring until the sugar is dissolved. Remove from heat and let cool.

In a medium bowl, whisk together the cooled syrup, lime juice, tequila, orange liqueur, and lime zest.

Pour the mixture into the KitchenAid Ice Cream Attachment.

Churn on low speed for 20-25 minutes, or until the mixture reaches a sorbet-like consistency.

Transfer the sorbet to a lidded container and freeze for at least 2 hours before serving.

Strawberry Champagne Sorbet

Servings: 8

Ingredients

- 4 cups fresh strawberries, hulled
- 1/2 cup granulated sugar
- 1/4 cup water
- 1 cup champagne
- 1 tablespoon fresh lemon juice

Instructions

In a blender or food processor, puree the strawberries until smooth.

In a medium bowl, whisk together the strawberry puree, sugar, water, champagne, and lemon juice until the sugar is completely dissolved.

Pour the mixture into the KitchenAid Ice Cream Attachment.

Churn on low speed for 20-25 minutes, or until the mixture reaches a sorbet-like consistency.

Transfer the sorbet to a lidded container and freeze for at least 2 hours before serving.

Spiked Eggnog Ice Cream

Servings: 8

Ingredients

- 2 cups heavy cream
- 1 cup whole milk
- 3/4 cup granulated sugar
- 1/2 cup eggnog
- 1/4 cup brandy or rum
- 1 teaspoon pure vanilla extract
- 1/2 teaspoon ground nutmeg

Instructions

In a medium bowl, whisk together the cream, milk, sugar, eggnog, brandy or rum, vanilla extract, and nutmeg until the sugar is completely dissolved.

Pour the mixture into the KitchenAid Ice Cream Attachment.

Churn on low speed for 25-30 minutes, or until the mixture reaches a soft-serve consistency.

Transfer the ice cream to a lidded container and freeze for at least 2 hours before serving.

Mojito Sorbet

Servings: 8

Ingredients

- 4 cups water
- 1 cup granulated sugar
- 1 cup fresh lime juice
- 1/2 cup white rum
- 1/4 cup fresh mint leaves, chopped

Instructions

In a saucepan, combine the water and sugar. Bring to a boil, stirring until the sugar is dissolved. Remove from heat and let cool.

In a medium bowl, whisk together the cooled syrup, lime juice, rum, and mint leaves.

Pour the mixture into the KitchenAid Ice Cream Attachment.

Churn on low speed for 20-25 minutes, or until the mixture reaches a sorbet-like consistency.

Transfer the sorbet to a lidded container and freeze for at least 2 hours before serving.

Amaretto Cherry Ice Cream

Servings: 8

Ingredients

- 2 cups heavy cream
- 1 cup whole milk
- 3/4 cup granulated sugar
- 1/2 cup Amaretto liqueur
- 1 cup fresh cherries, pitted and halved
- 1 teaspoon pure vanilla extract

Instructions

In a medium bowl, whisk together the cream, milk, sugar, Amaretto, cherries, and vanilla extract until the sugar is completely dissolved.

Pour the mixture into the KitchenAid Ice Cream Attachment.

Churn on low speed for 25-30 minutes, or until the mixture reaches a soft-serve consistency.

Transfer the ice cream to a lidded container and freeze for at least 2 hours before serving.

Bailey's Chocolate Chip Ice Cream

Servings: 8

Ingredients

- 2 cups heavy cream
- 1 cup whole milk
- 3/4 cup granulated sugar
- 1/2 cup Bailey's Irish Cream
- 1 teaspoon pure vanilla extract
- 1 cup mini chocolate chips

Instructions

In a medium bowl, whisk together the cream, milk, sugar, Bailey's, and vanilla extract until the sugar is completely dissolved.

Stir in the mini chocolate chips.

Pour the mixture into the KitchenAid Ice Cream Attachment.

Churn on low speed for 25-30 minutes, or until the mixture reaches a soft-serve consistency.

Transfer the ice cream to a lidded container and freeze for at least 2 hours before serving.

Kahlua Espresso Ice Cream

Servings: 8

Ingredients

- 2 cups heavy cream
- 1 cup whole milk
- 3/4 cup granulated sugar
- 1/2 cup Kahlua
- 1/4 cup strong brewed espresso, cooled
- 1 teaspoon pure vanilla extract

Instructions

In a medium bowl, whisk together the cream, milk, sugar, Kahlua, espresso, and vanilla extract until the sugar is completely dissolved.

Pour the mixture into the KitchenAid Ice Cream Attachment.

Churn on low speed for 25-30 minutes, or until the mixture reaches a soft-serve consistency.

Transfer the ice cream to a lidded container and freeze for at least 2 hours before serving.

Spiced Rum Ice Cream

Servings: 8

Ingredients

- 2 cups heavy cream
- 1 cup whole milk
- 3/4 cup granulated sugar
- 1/2 cup spiced rum
- 1 teaspoon pure vanilla extract
- 1/2 teaspoon ground cinnamon
- 1/4 teaspoon ground nutmeg

Instructions

In a medium bowl, whisk together the cream, milk, sugar, spiced rum, vanilla extract, cinnamon, and nutmeg until the sugar is completely dissolved.

Pour the mixture into the KitchenAid Ice Cream Attachment.

Churn on low speed for 25-30 minutes, or until the mixture reaches a soft-serve consistency.

Transfer the ice cream to a lidded container and freeze for at least 2 hours before serving.

Mint Julep Ice Cream

Servings: 8

Ingredients

- 2 cups heavy cream
- 1 cup whole milk
- 3/4 cup granulated sugar
- 1/2 cup bourbon
- 1/4 cup fresh mint leaves, chopped
- 1 teaspoon pure vanilla extract

Instructions

In a medium bowl, whisk together the cream, milk, sugar, bourbon, mint leaves, and vanilla extract until the sugar is completely dissolved.

Pour the mixture into the KitchenAid Ice Cream Attachment.

Churn on low speed for 25-30 minutes, or until the mixture reaches a soft-serve consistency.

Transfer the ice cream to a lidded container and freeze for at least 2 hours before serving.

Apple Brandy Ice Cream

Servings: 8

Ingredients

- 2 cups heavy cream
- 1 cup whole milk
- 3/4 cup granulated sugar
- 1/2 cup apple brandy
- 1 teaspoon pure vanilla extract
- 1/2 teaspoon ground cinnamon

Instructions

In a medium bowl, whisk together the cream, milk, sugar, apple brandy, vanilla extract, and cinnamon until the sugar is completely dissolved.

Pour the mixture into the KitchenAid Ice Cream Attachment.

Churn on low speed for 25-30 minutes, or until the mixture reaches a soft-serve consistency.

Transfer the ice cream to a lidded container and freeze for at least 2 hours before serving.

Dark Chocolate Stout Ice Cream

Servings: 8

Ingredients

- 2 cups heavy cream
- 1 cup whole milk
- 3/4 cup granulated sugar
- 1/2 cup stout beer
- 1/2 cup dark chocolate, melted
- 1 teaspoon pure vanilla extract

Instructions

In a medium bowl, whisk together the cream, milk, sugar, stout beer, melted dark chocolate, and vanilla extract until the sugar is completely dissolved.

Pour the mixture into the KitchenAid Ice Cream Attachment.

Churn on low speed for 25-30 minutes, or until the mixture reaches a soft-serve consistency.

Transfer the ice cream to a lidded container and freeze for at least 2 hours before serving.

Tequila Lime Ice Cream

Servings: 8

Ingredients

- 2 cups heavy cream
- 1 cup whole milk
- 3/4 cup granulated sugar
- 1/2 cup tequila
- 1/4 cup fresh lime juice
- 1 teaspoon pure vanilla extract

Instructions

In a medium bowl, whisk together the cream, milk, sugar, tequila, lime juice, and vanilla extract until the sugar is completely dissolved.

Pour the mixture into the KitchenAid Ice Cream Attachment.

Churn on low speed for 25-30 minutes, or until the mixture reaches a soft-serve consistency.

Transfer the ice cream to a lidded container and freeze for at least 2 hours before serving.

Gin and Tonic Sorbet

Servings: 8

Ingredients

- 4 cups water
- 1 cup granulated sugar
- 1 cup tonic water
- 1/2 cup gin
- 1/4 cup fresh lime juice
- 1 tablespoon lime zest

Instructions

In a saucepan, combine the water and sugar. Bring to a boil, stirring until the sugar is dissolved. Remove from heat and let cool.

In a medium bowl, whisk together the cooled syrup, tonic water, gin, lime juice, and lime zest.

Pour the mixture into the KitchenAid Ice Cream Attachment.

Churn on low speed for 20-25 minutes, or until the mixture reaches a sorbet-like consistency.

Transfer the sorbet to a lidded container and freeze for at least 2 hours before serving.

Cherry Amaretto Ice Cream

Servings: 8

Ingredients

- 2 cups heavy cream
- 1 cup whole milk
- 3/4 cup granulated sugar
- 1/2 cup Amaretto liqueur
- 1 cup fresh cherries, pitted and halved
- 1 teaspoon pure vanilla extract

Instructions

In a medium bowl, whisk together the cream, milk, sugar, Amaretto, cherries, and vanilla extract until the sugar is completely dissolved.

Pour the mixture into the KitchenAid Ice Cream Attachment.

Churn on low speed for 25-30 minutes, or until the mixture reaches a soft-serve consistency.

Transfer the ice cream to a lidded container and freeze for at least 2 hours before serving.

Spiced Apple Cider Ice Cream

Servings: 8

Ingredients

- 2 cups heavy cream
- 1 cup whole milk
- 3/4 cup granulated sugar
- 1/2 cup apple cider
- 1/4 cup spiced rum
- 1 teaspoon pure vanilla extract
- 1/2 teaspoon ground cinnamon
- 1/4 teaspoon ground nutmeg

Instructions

In a medium bowl, whisk together the cream, milk, sugar, apple cider, spiced rum, vanilla extract, cinnamon, and nutmeg until the sugar is completely dissolved.

Pour the mixture into the KitchenAid Ice Cream Attachment.

Churn on low speed for 25-30 minutes, or until the mixture reaches a soft-serve consistency.

Transfer the ice cream to a lidded container and freeze for at least 2 hours before serving.

Coconut Rum Ice Cream

Servings: 8

Ingredients

- 2 cups coconut milk
- 1 cup heavy cream
- 3/4 cup granulated sugar
- 1/2 cup coconut rum
- 1 teaspoon pure vanilla extract

Instructions

In a medium bowl, whisk together the coconut milk, cream, sugar, coconut rum, and vanilla extract until the sugar is completely dissolved.

Pour the mixture into the KitchenAid Ice Cream Attachment.

Churn on low speed for 25-30 minutes, or until the mixture reaches a soft-serve consistency.

Transfer the ice cream to a lidded container and freeze for at least 2 hours before serving.

Champagne Peach Ice Cream

Servings: 8

Ingredients

- 2 cups heavy cream
- 1 cup whole milk
- 3/4 cup granulated sugar
- 1 cup champagne
- 1 cup fresh peaches, peeled and diced
- 1 teaspoon pure vanilla extract

Instructions

In a medium bowl, whisk together the cream, milk, sugar, champagne, peaches, and vanilla extract until the sugar is completely dissolved.

Pour the mixture into the KitchenAid Ice Cream Attachment.

Churn on low speed for 25-30 minutes, or until the mixture reaches a soft-serve consistency.

Transfer the ice cream to a lidded container and freeze for at least 2 hours before serving.

Maple Bourbon Pecan Ice Cream

Servings: 8

Ingredients

- 2 cups heavy cream
- 1 cup whole milk
- 3/4 cup granulated sugar
- 1/2 cup maple syrup
- 1/4 cup bourbon
- 1 teaspoon pure vanilla extract
- 1 cup toasted pecans, chopped

Instructions

In a medium bowl, whisk together the cream, milk, sugar, maple syrup, bourbon, and vanilla extract until the sugar is completely dissolved.

Stir in the chopped pecans.

Pour the mixture into the KitchenAid Ice Cream Attachment.

Churn on low speed for 25-30 minutes, or until the mixture reaches a soft-serve consistency.

Transfer the ice cream to a lidded container and freeze for at least 2 hours before serving.

White Russian Ice Cream

Servings: 8

Ingredients

- 2 cups heavy cream
- 1 cup whole milk
- 3/4 cup granulated sugar
- 1/2 cup vodka
- 1/2 cup Kahlua
- 1 teaspoon pure vanilla extract

Instructions

In a medium bowl, whisk together the cream, milk, sugar, vodka, Kahlua, and vanilla extract until the sugar is completely dissolved.

Pour the mixture into the KitchenAid Ice Cream Attachment.

Churn on low speed for 25-30 minutes, or until the mixture reaches a soft-serve consistency.

Transfer the ice cream to a lidded container and freeze for at least 2 hours before serving.

Sangria Sorbet

Servings: 8

Ingredients

- 4 cups red wine
- 1 cup granulated sugar
- 1 cup orange juice
- 1/2 cup brandy
- 1/2 cup fresh strawberries, sliced
- 1/2 cup fresh peaches, diced

Instructions

In a medium bowl, whisk together the wine, sugar, orange juice, brandy, strawberries, and peaches until the sugar is completely dissolved.

Pour the mixture into the KitchenAid Ice Cream Attachment.

Churn on low speed for 20-25 minutes, or until the mixture reaches a sorbet-like consistency.

Transfer the sorbet to a lidded container and freeze for at least 2 hours before serving.

Brandy Alexander Ice Cream

Servings: 8

Ingredients

- 2 cups heavy cream
- 1 cup whole milk
- 3/4 cup granulated sugar
- 1/2 cup brandy
- 1/2 cup crème de cacao
- 1 teaspoon pure vanilla extract

Instructions

In a medium bowl, whisk together the cream, milk, sugar, brandy, crème de cacao, and vanilla extract until the sugar is completely dissolved.

Pour the mixture into the KitchenAid Ice Cream Attachment.

Churn on low speed for 25-30 minutes, or until the mixture reaches a soft-serve consistency.

Transfer the ice cream to a lidded container and freeze for at least 2 hours before serving.

Blackberry Merlot Sorbet

Servings: 8

Ingredients

- 4 cups fresh blackberries
- 1/2 cup granulated sugar
- 1/4 cup water
- 1 cup Merlot wine
- 1 tablespoon fresh lemon juice

Instructions

In a blender or food processor, puree the blackberries until smooth. Strain through a fine-mesh sieve to remove the seeds.

In a medium bowl, whisk together the blackberry puree, sugar, water, Merlot, and lemon juice until the sugar is completely dissolved.

Pour the mixture into the KitchenAid Ice Cream Attachment.

Churn on low speed for 20-25 minutes, or until the mixture reaches a sorbet-like consistency.

Transfer the sorbet to a lidded container and freeze for at least 2 hours before serving.

Gin Basil Ice Cream

Servings: 8

Ingredients

- 2 cups heavy cream
- 1 cup whole milk
- 3/4 cup granulated sugar
- 1/2 cup gin
- 1/4 cup fresh basil leaves, chopped
- 1 teaspoon pure vanilla extract

Instructions

In a medium bowl, whisk together the cream, milk, sugar, gin, basil, and vanilla extract until the sugar is completely dissolved.

Pour the mixture into the KitchenAid Ice Cream Attachment.

Churn on low speed for 25-30 minutes, or until the mixture reaches a soft-serve consistency.

Transfer the ice cream to a lidded container and freeze for at least 2 hours before serving.

Caramel Whiskey Ice Cream

Servings: 8

Ingredients

- 2 cups heavy cream
- 1 cup whole milk
- 3/4 cup granulated sugar
- 1/2 cup caramel sauce
- 1/4 cup whiskey
- 1 teaspoon pure vanilla extract

Instructions

In a medium bowl, whisk together the cream, milk, sugar, caramel sauce, whiskey, and vanilla extract until the sugar is completely dissolved.

Pour the mixture into the KitchenAid Ice Cream Attachment.

Churn on low speed for 25-30 minutes, or until the mixture reaches a soft-serve consistency.

Transfer the ice cream to a lidded container and freeze for at least 2 hours before serving.

Coconut Pineapple Rum Sorbet

Servings: 8

Ingredients

- 4 cups fresh pineapple, diced
- 1/2 cup coconut milk
- 1/2 cup granulated sugar
- 1/4 cup water
- 1/2 cup white rum
- 1 tablespoon fresh lime juice

Instructions

In a blender or food processor, puree the pineapple until smooth.

In a medium bowl, whisk together the pineapple puree, coconut milk, sugar, water, rum, and lime juice until the sugar is completely dissolved.

Pour the mixture into the KitchenAid Ice Cream Attachment.

Churn on low speed for 20-25 minutes, or until the mixture reaches a sorbet-like consistency.

Transfer the sorbet to a lidded container and freeze for at least 2 hours before serving.

Raspberry Prosecco Sorbet

Servings: 8

Ingredients

- 4 cups fresh raspberries
- 1/2 cup granulated sugar
- 1/4 cup water
- 1 cup Prosecco
- 1 tablespoon fresh lemon juice

Instructions

In a blender or food processor, puree the raspberries until smooth. Strain through a fine-mesh sieve to remove the seeds.

In a medium bowl, whisk together the raspberry puree, sugar, water, Prosecco, and lemon juice until the sugar is completely dissolved.

Pour the mixture into the KitchenAid Ice Cream Attachment.

Churn on low speed for 20-25 minutes, or until the mixture reaches a sorbet-like consistency.

Transfer the sorbet to a lidded container and freeze for at least 2 hours before serving.

7. Ice Cream Sandwiches and Other Treats

Classic Chocolate Chip Cookie Ice Cream Sandwich

Servings: 8 sandwiches

Ingredients

For the Ice Cream:

- 2 cups heavy cream
- 1 cup whole milk
- 3/4 cup granulated sugar
- 1 teaspoon pure vanilla extract

For the Cookies:

- 1 cup unsalted butter, softened
- 3/4 cup granulated sugar
- 3/4 cup brown sugar, packed
- 2 large eggs
- 2 teaspoons pure vanilla extract
- 2 1/4 cups all-purpose flour
- 1 teaspoon baking soda
- 1/2 teaspoon salt
- 2 cups chocolate chips

Instructions

Make the Ice Cream:

In a medium bowl, whisk together the cream, milk, sugar, and vanilla extract until the sugar is completely dissolved.

Pour the mixture into the KitchenAid Ice Cream Attachment.

Churn on low speed for 25-30 minutes, or until the mixture reaches a soft-serve consistency.

Transfer the ice cream to a lidded container and freeze for at least 2 hours.

Make the Cookies:

Preheat the oven to 350°F (175°C).

In a large bowl, cream together the butter and sugars until light and fluffy. Beat in the eggs and vanilla until well combined.

In another bowl, whisk together the flour, baking soda, and salt. Gradually add the dry ingredients to the wet ingredients, mixing until just combined. Stir in the chocolate chips.

Drop tablespoon-sized balls of dough onto a baking sheet lined with parchment paper, spacing them about 2 inches apart. Flatten slightly with your hand.

Bake for 10-12 minutes, or until the edges are golden brown. Let cool completely.

Assemble the Sandwiches:

Scoop a generous amount of ice cream onto the flat side of one cookie. Top with another cookie, flat side down, and press gently to spread the ice cream evenly.

Wrap each sandwich in plastic wrap and freeze for at least 1 hour before serving.

Caramel Apple Ice Cream Sandwich

Servings: 8 sandwiches

Ingredients

For the Ice Cream:

- 2 cups heavy cream
- 1 cup whole milk
- 3/4 cup granulated sugar
- 1 teaspoon pure vanilla extract
- 1/2 cup caramel sauce
- 1/2 cup finely chopped apples

For the Cookies:

- 1 cup unsalted butter, softened
- 1 cup granulated sugar
- 1/2 cup brown sugar, packed
- 2 large eggs
- 2 teaspoons pure vanilla extract
- 2 1/2 cups all-purpose flour
- 1 teaspoon baking soda
- 1/2 teaspoon salt
- 1 teaspoon ground cinnamon
- 1/2 cup finely chopped dried apples

Instructions

Make the Ice Cream:

In a medium bowl, whisk together the cream, milk, sugar, vanilla extract, and caramel sauce until the sugar is completely dissolved. Stir in the finely chopped apples.

Pour the mixture into the KitchenAid Ice Cream Attachment.

Churn on low speed for 25-30 minutes, or until the mixture reaches a soft-serve consistency.

Transfer the ice cream to a lidded container and freeze for at least 2 hours.

Make the Cookies:

Preheat the oven to 350°F (175°C).

In a large bowl, cream together the butter and sugars until light and fluffy. Beat in the eggs and vanilla until well combined.

In another bowl, whisk together the flour, baking soda, salt, and cinnamon. Gradually add the dry ingredients to the wet ingredients, mixing until just combined. Stir in the chopped dried apples.

Drop tablespoon-sized balls of dough onto a baking sheet lined with parchment paper, spacing them about 2 inches apart. Flatten slightly with your hand.

Bake for 10-12 minutes, or until the edges are golden brown. Let cool completely.

Assemble the Sandwiches:

Scoop a generous amount of ice cream onto the flat side of one cookie. Top with another cookie, flat side down, and press gently to spread the ice cream evenly.

Wrap each sandwich in plastic wrap and freeze for at least 1 hour before serving.

Peanut Butter Cookie Ice Cream Sandwich

Servings: 8 sandwiches

Ingredients

For the Ice Cream:

- 2 cups heavy cream
- 1 cup whole milk
- 3/4 cup granulated sugar
- 1 teaspoon pure vanilla extract
- 1/2 cup peanut butter

For the Cookies:

- 1 cup unsalted butter, softened
- 1 cup peanut butter
- 1 cup granulated sugar
- 1 cup brown sugar, packed
- 2 large eggs
- 2 teaspoons pure vanilla extract
- 2 1/2 cups all-purpose flour
- 1 teaspoon baking soda
- 1/2 teaspoon salt

Instructions

Make the Ice Cream:

In a medium bowl, whisk together the cream, milk, sugar, vanilla extract, and peanut butter until smooth and the sugar is completely dissolved.

Pour the mixture into the KitchenAid Ice Cream Attachment.

Churn on low speed for 25-30 minutes, or until the mixture reaches a soft-serve consistency.

Transfer the ice cream to a lidded container and freeze for at least 2 hours.

Make the Cookies:

Preheat the oven to 350°F (175°C).

In a large bowl, cream together the butter, peanut butter, and sugars until light and fluffy. Beat in the eggs and vanilla until well combined.

In another bowl, whisk together the flour, baking soda, and salt. Gradually add the dry ingredients to the wet ingredients, mixing until just combined.

Drop tablespoon-sized balls of dough onto a baking sheet lined with parchment paper, spacing them about 2 inches apart. Flatten slightly with a fork.

Bake for 10-12 minutes, or until the edges are golden brown. Let cool completely.

Assemble the Sandwiches:

Scoop a generous amount of ice cream onto the flat side of one cookie. Top with another cookie, flat side down, and press gently to spread the ice cream evenly.

Wrap each sandwich in plastic wrap and freeze for at least 1 hour before serving.

Brownie Ice Cream Sandwich

Servings: 8 sandwiches

Ingredients

For the Ice Cream:

- 2 cups heavy cream
- 1 cup whole milk
- 3/4 cup granulated sugar
- 1 teaspoon pure vanilla extract
- 1/2 cup unsweetened cocoa powder

For the Brownies:

- 1/2 cup unsalted butter, melted

- 1 cup granulated sugar
- 2 large eggs
- 1 teaspoon pure vanilla extract
- 1/3 cup unsweetened cocoa powder
- 1/2 cup all-purpose flour
- 1/4 teaspoon salt
- 1/4 teaspoon baking powder

Instructions

Make the Ice Cream:

In a medium bowl, whisk together the cream, milk, sugar, vanilla extract, and cocoa powder until the sugar is completely dissolved.

Pour the mixture into the KitchenAid Ice Cream Attachment.

Churn on low speed for 25-30 minutes, or until the mixture reaches a soft-serve consistency.

Transfer the ice cream to a lidded container and freeze for at least 2 hours.

Make the Brownies:

Preheat the oven to 350°F (175°C).

In a large bowl, mix together the melted butter and sugar until well combined. Beat in the eggs and vanilla until smooth.

In another bowl, whisk together the cocoa powder, flour, salt, and baking powder. Gradually add the dry ingredients to the wet ingredients, mixing until just combined.

Spread the batter into a greased and parchment-lined 9x13 inch baking pan.

Bake for 20-25 minutes, or until a toothpick inserted into the center comes out clean. Let cool completely.

Cut the brownies into squares to match the size of the sandwiches you desire.

Assemble the Sandwiches:

Scoop a generous amount of ice cream onto one brownie square. Top with another brownie square and press gently to spread the ice cream evenly.

Wrap each sandwich in plastic wrap and freeze for at least 1 hour before serving.

Lemon Sugar Cookie Ice Cream Sandwich

Servings: 8 sandwiches

Ingredients

For the Ice Cream:

- 2 cups heavy cream
- 1 cup whole milk
- 3/4 cup granulated sugar
- 1 teaspoon pure vanilla extract
- 1 tablespoon lemon zest

For the Cookies:

- 1 cup unsalted butter, softened
- 1 cup granulated sugar
- 1 large egg
- 2 teaspoons pure vanilla extract
- 2 1/2 cups all-purpose flour
- 1 teaspoon baking powder
- 1/2 teaspoon salt
- 1 tablespoon lemon zest

Instructions

Make the Ice Cream:

In a medium bowl, whisk together the cream, milk, sugar, vanilla extract, and lemon zest until the sugar is completely dissolved.

Pour the mixture into the KitchenAid Ice Cream Attachment.

Churn on low speed for 25-30 minutes, or until the mixture reaches a soft-serve consistency.

Transfer the ice cream to a lidded container and freeze for at least 2 hours.

Make the Cookies:

Preheat the oven to 350°F (175°C).

In a large bowl, cream together the butter and sugar until light and fluffy. Beat in the egg and vanilla until well combined.

In another bowl, whisk together the flour, baking powder, salt, and lemon zest. Gradually add the dry ingredients to the wet ingredients, mixing until just combined.

Drop tablespoon-sized balls of dough onto a baking sheet lined with parchment paper, spacing them about 2 inches apart. Flatten slightly with your hand.

Bake for 10-12 minutes, or until the edges are golden brown. Let cool completely.

Assemble the Sandwiches:

Scoop a generous amount of ice cream onto the flat side of one cookie. Top with another cookie, flat side down, and press gently to spread the ice cream evenly.

Wrap each sandwich in plastic wrap and freeze for at least 1 hour before serving.

Red Velvet Cookie Ice Cream Sandwich

Servings: 8 sandwiches

Ingredients

For the Ice Cream:

2 cups heavy cream

1 cup whole milk

3/4 cup granulated sugar

1 teaspoon pure vanilla extract

For the Cookies:

1 cup unsalted butter, softened

1 cup granulated sugar

1 cup brown sugar, packed

2 large eggs

1 teaspoon pure vanilla extract

1 tablespoon red food coloring

2 1/2 cups all-purpose flour

1/4 cup unsweetened cocoa powder

1 teaspoon baking soda

1/2 teaspoon salt

1 cup white chocolate chips

Instructions

Make the Ice Cream:

In a medium bowl, whisk together the cream, milk, sugar, and vanilla extract until the sugar is completely dissolved.

Pour the mixture into the KitchenAid Ice Cream Attachment.

Churn on low speed for 25-30 minutes, or until the mixture reaches a soft-serve consistency.

Transfer the ice cream to a lidded container and freeze for at least 2 hours.

Make the Cookies:

Preheat the oven to 350°F (175°C).

In a large bowl, cream together the butter and sugars until light and fluffy. Beat in the eggs, vanilla, and red food coloring until well combined.

In another bowl, whisk together the flour, cocoa powder, baking soda, and salt. Gradually add the dry ingredients to the wet ingredients, mixing until just combined. Stir in the white chocolate chips.

Drop tablespoon-sized balls of dough onto a baking sheet lined with parchment paper, spacing them about 2 inches apart. Flatten slightly with your hand.

Bake for 10-12 minutes, or until the edges are golden brown. Let cool completely.

Assemble the Sandwiches:

Scoop a generous amount of ice cream onto the flat side of one cookie. Top with another cookie, flat side down, and press gently to spread the ice cream evenly.

Wrap each sandwich in plastic wrap and freeze for at least 1 hour before serving.

Oatmeal Raisin Cookie Ice Cream Sandwich

Servings: 8 sandwiches

Ingredients

For the Ice Cream:

- 2 cups heavy cream
- 1 cup whole milk
- 3/4 cup granulated sugar
- 1 teaspoon pure vanilla extract
- 1/2 teaspoon ground cinnamon

For the Cookies:

- 1 cup unsalted butter, softened
- 1 cup granulated sugar
- 1 cup brown sugar, packed

- 2 large eggs
- 2 teaspoons pure vanilla extract
- 2 cups all-purpose flour
- 1 teaspoon baking soda
- 1/2 teaspoon salt
- 1 teaspoon ground cinnamon
- 3 cups old-fashioned rolled oats
- 1 cup raisins

Instructions

Make the Ice Cream:

In a medium bowl, whisk together the cream, milk, sugar, vanilla extract, and cinnamon until the sugar is completely dissolved.

Pour the mixture into the KitchenAid Ice Cream Attachment.

Churn on low speed for 25-30 minutes, or until the mixture reaches a soft-serve consistency.

Transfer the ice cream to a lidded container and freeze for at least 2 hours.

Make the Cookies:

Preheat the oven to 350°F (175°C).

In a large bowl, cream together the butter and sugars until light and fluffy. Beat in the eggs and vanilla until well combined.

In another bowl, whisk together the flour, baking soda, salt, and cinnamon. Gradually add the dry ingredients to the wet ingredients, mixing until just combined. Stir in the oats and raisins.

Drop tablespoon-sized balls of dough onto a baking sheet lined with parchment paper, spacing them about 2 inches apart. Flatten slightly with your hand.

Bake for 10-12 minutes, or until the edges are golden brown. Let cool completely.

Assemble the Sandwiches:

Scoop a generous amount of ice cream onto the flat side of one cookie. Top with another cookie, flat side down, and press gently to spread the ice cream evenly.

Wrap each sandwich in plastic wrap and freeze for at least 1 hour before serving.

Sugar Cookie Ice Cream Sandwich

Servings: 8 sandwiches

Ingredients

For the Ice Cream:

- 2 cups heavy cream
- 1 cup whole milk
- 3/4 cup granulated sugar
- 1 teaspoon pure vanilla extract

For the Cookies:

- 1 cup unsalted butter, softened
- 1 cup granulated sugar
- 1 large egg
- 2 teaspoons pure vanilla extract
- 2 1/2 cups all-purpose flour
- 1 teaspoon baking powder
- 1/2 teaspoon salt
- Sprinkles for decorating (optional)

Instructions

Make the Ice Cream:

In a medium bowl, whisk together the cream, milk, sugar, and vanilla extract until the sugar is completely dissolved.

Pour the mixture into the KitchenAid Ice Cream Attachment.

Churn on low speed for 25-30 minutes, or until the mixture reaches a soft-serve consistency.

Transfer the ice cream to a lidded container and freeze for at least 2 hours.

Make the Cookies:

Preheat the oven to 350°F (175°C).

In a large bowl, cream together the butter and sugar until light and fluffy. Beat in the egg and vanilla until well combined.

In another bowl, whisk together the flour, baking powder, and salt. Gradually add the dry ingredients to the wet ingredients, mixing until just combined.

Drop tablespoon-sized balls of dough onto a baking sheet lined with parchment paper, spacing them about 2 inches apart. Flatten slightly with your hand. Add sprinkles on top, if desired.

Bake for 10-12 minutes, or until the edges are golden brown. Let cool completely.

Assemble the Sandwiches:

Scoop a generous amount of ice cream onto the flat side of one cookie. Top with another cookie, flat side down, and press gently to spread the ice cream evenly.

Wrap each sandwich in plastic wrap and freeze for at least 1 hour before serving.

Snickerdoodle Ice Cream Sandwich

Servings: 8 sandwiches

Ingredients

For the Ice Cream:

- 2 cups heavy cream

- 1 cup whole milk
- 3/4 cup granulated sugar
- 1 teaspoon pure vanilla extract
- 1 teaspoon ground cinnamon

For the Cookies:

- 1 cup unsalted butter, softened
- 1 cup granulated sugar
- 1/2 cup brown sugar, packed
- 2 large eggs
- 2 teaspoons pure vanilla extract
- 2 1/2 cups all-purpose flour
- 1 teaspoon baking soda
- 1/2 teaspoon salt
- 1 teaspoon ground cinnamon
- 1/4 cup granulated sugar (for rolling)
- 1 tablespoon ground cinnamon (for rolling)

Instructions

Make the Ice Cream:

In a medium bowl, whisk together the cream, milk, sugar, vanilla extract, and cinnamon until the sugar is completely dissolved.

Pour the mixture into the KitchenAid Ice Cream Attachment.

Churn on low speed for 25-30 minutes, or until the mixture reaches a soft-serve consistency.

Transfer the ice cream to a lidded container and freeze for at least 2 hours.

Make the Cookies:

Preheat the oven to 350°F (175°C).

In a large bowl, cream together the butter and sugars until light and fluffy. Beat in the eggs and vanilla until well combined.

In another bowl, whisk together the flour, baking soda, salt, and cinnamon. Gradually add the dry ingredients to the wet ingredients, mixing until just combined.

In a small bowl, mix together the granulated sugar and cinnamon for rolling.

Drop tablespoon-sized balls of dough into the cinnamon sugar mixture, coating them completely, then place onto a baking sheet lined with parchment paper, spacing them about 2 inches apart. Flatten slightly with your hand.

Bake for 10-12 minutes, or until the edges are golden brown. Let cool completely.

Assemble the Sandwiches:

Scoop a generous amount of ice cream onto the flat side of one cookie. Top with another cookie, flat side down, and press gently to spread the ice cream evenly.

Wrap each sandwich in plastic wrap and freeze for at least 1 hour before serving.

Chocolate Peppermint Patty Ice Cream Sandwich

Servings: 8 sandwiches

Ingredients

For the Ice Cream:

- 2 cups heavy cream
- 1 cup whole milk
- 3/4 cup granulated sugar
- 1 teaspoon pure vanilla extract
- 1/2 teaspoon peppermint extract
- 1/2 cup crushed peppermint candies

For the Cookies:

- 1 cup unsalted butter, softened
- 1 cup granulated sugar

- 1 cup brown sugar, packed
- 2 large eggs
- 2 teaspoons pure vanilla extract
- 2 cups all-purpose flour
- 1/2 cup unsweetened cocoa powder
- 1 teaspoon baking soda
- 1/2 teaspoon salt

Instructions

Make the Ice Cream:

In a medium bowl, whisk together the cream, milk, sugar, vanilla extract, and peppermint extract until the sugar is completely dissolved.

Pour the mixture into the KitchenAid Ice Cream Attachment.

Churn on low speed for 25-30 minutes, or until the mixture reaches a soft-serve consistency.

Stir in the crushed peppermint candies.

Transfer the ice cream to a lidded container and freeze for at least 2 hours.

Make the Cookies:

Preheat the oven to 350°F (175°C).

In a large bowl, cream together the butter and sugars until light and fluffy. Beat in the eggs and vanilla until well combined.

In another bowl, whisk together the flour, cocoa powder, baking soda, and salt. Gradually add the dry ingredients to the wet ingredients, mixing until just combined.

Drop tablespoon-sized balls of dough onto a baking sheet lined with parchment paper, spacing them about 2 inches apart. Flatten slightly with your hand.

Bake for 10-12 minutes, or until the edges are golden brown. Let cool completely.

Assemble the Sandwiches:

Scoop a generous amount of ice cream onto the flat side of one cookie. Top with another cookie, flat side down, and press gently to spread the ice cream evenly.

Wrap each sandwich in plastic wrap and freeze for at least 1 hour before serving.

Coconut Macaroon Ice Cream Sandwich

Servings: 8 sandwiches

Ingredients

For the Ice Cream:

- 2 cups coconut milk
- 1 cup heavy cream
- 3/4 cup granulated sugar
- 1 teaspoon pure vanilla extract
- 1/2 cup shredded coconut

For the Cookies:

- 3 cups sweetened shredded coconut
- 3/4 cup sweetened condensed milk
- 1 teaspoon pure vanilla extract
- 2 large egg whites
- 1/4 teaspoon salt

Instructions

Make the Ice Cream:

In a medium bowl, whisk together the coconut milk, heavy cream, sugar, and vanilla extract until the sugar is completely dissolved. Stir in the shredded coconut.

Pour the mixture into the KitchenAid Ice Cream Attachment.

Churn on low speed for 25-30 minutes, or until the mixture reaches a soft-serve consistency.

Transfer the ice cream to a lidded container and freeze for at least 2 hours.

Make the Cookies:

Preheat the oven to 325°F (165°C).

In a large bowl, mix together the shredded coconut, sweetened condensed milk, and vanilla extract until well combined.

In another bowl, beat the egg whites and salt until stiff peaks form. Gently fold the egg whites into the coconut mixture.

Drop tablespoon-sized balls of dough onto a baking sheet lined with parchment paper, spacing them about 2 inches apart. Flatten slightly with your hand.

Bake for 20-25 minutes, or until the edges are golden brown. Let cool completely.

Assemble the Sandwiches:

Scoop a generous amount of ice cream onto the flat side of one cookie. Top with another cookie, flat side down, and press gently to spread the ice cream evenly.

Wrap each sandwich in plastic wrap and freeze for at least 1 hour before serving.

S'mores Ice Cream Sandwich

Servings: 8 sandwiches

Ingredients

For the Ice Cream:

- 2 cups heavy cream
- 1 cup whole milk
- 3/4 cup granulated sugar
- 1 teaspoon pure vanilla extract
- 1 cup mini marshmallows

For the Cookies:

- 1 cup unsalted butter, softened
- 3/4 cup granulated sugar
- 3/4 cup brown sugar, packed
- 2 large eggs
- 2 teaspoons pure vanilla extract
- 2 1/2 cups all-purpose flour
- 1 teaspoon baking soda
- 1/2 teaspoon salt
- 1 cup graham cracker crumbs
- 1 cup chocolate chips

Instructions

Make the Ice Cream:

In a medium bowl, whisk together the cream, milk, sugar, and vanilla extract until the sugar is completely dissolved.

Pour the mixture into the KitchenAid Ice Cream Attachment.

Churn on low speed for 25-30 minutes, or until the mixture reaches a soft-serve consistency.

Stir in the mini marshmallows.

Transfer the ice cream to a lidded container and freeze for at least 2 hours.

Make the Cookies:

Preheat the oven to 350°F (175°C).

In a large bowl, cream together the butter and sugars until light and fluffy. Beat in the eggs and vanilla until well combined.

In another bowl, whisk together the flour, baking soda, salt, and graham cracker crumbs. Gradually add the dry ingredients to the wet ingredients, mixing until just combined. Stir in the chocolate chips.

Drop tablespoon-sized balls of dough onto a baking sheet lined with parchment paper, spacing them about 2 inches apart. Flatten slightly with your hand.

Bake for 10-12 minutes, or until the edges are golden brown. Let cool completely.

Assemble the Sandwiches:

Scoop a generous amount of ice cream onto the flat side of one cookie. Top with another cookie, flat side down, and press gently to spread the ice cream evenly.

Wrap each sandwich in plastic wrap and freeze for at least 1 hour before serving.

Matcha Green Tea Ice Cream Sandwich

Servings: 8 sandwiches

Ingredients

For the Ice Cream:

- 2 cups heavy cream
- 1 cup whole milk
- 3/4 cup granulated sugar
- 1 teaspoon pure vanilla extract
- 2 tablespoons matcha green tea powder

For the Cookies:

- 1 cup unsalted butter, softened
- 1 cup granulated sugar
- 1 large egg
- 2 teaspoons pure vanilla extract
- 2 1/2 cups all-purpose flour
- 1 teaspoon baking powder
- 1/2 teaspoon salt
- 1 tablespoon matcha green tea powder

Instructions

Make the Ice Cream:

In a medium bowl, whisk together the cream, milk, sugar, vanilla extract, and matcha powder until the sugar is completely dissolved.

Pour the mixture into the KitchenAid Ice Cream Attachment.

Churn on low speed for 25-30 minutes, or until the mixture reaches a soft-serve consistency.

Transfer the ice cream to a lidded container and freeze for at least 2 hours.

Make the Cookies:

Preheat the oven to 350°F (175°C).

In a large bowl, cream together the butter and sugar until light and fluffy. Beat in the egg and vanilla until well combined.

In another bowl, whisk together the flour, baking powder, salt, and matcha powder. Gradually add the dry ingredients to the wet ingredients, mixing until just combined.

Drop tablespoon-sized balls of dough onto a baking sheet lined with parchment paper, spacing them about 2 inches apart. Flatten slightly with your hand.

Bake for 10-12 minutes, or until the edges are golden brown. Let cool completely.

Assemble the Sandwiches:

Scoop a generous amount of ice cream onto the flat side of one cookie. Top with another cookie, flat side down, and press gently to spread the ice cream evenly.

Wrap each sandwich in plastic wrap and freeze for at least 1 hour before serving.

Pumpkin Spice Ice Cream Sandwich

Servings: 8 sandwiches

Ingredients

For the Ice Cream:

- 2 cups heavy cream
- 1 cup whole milk
- 3/4 cup granulated sugar
- 1 teaspoon pure vanilla extract
- 1 cup pumpkin puree
- 1 teaspoon pumpkin pie spice

For the Cookies:

- 1 cup unsalted butter, softened
- 1 cup granulated sugar
- 1/2 cup brown sugar, packed
- 2 large eggs
- 2 teaspoons pure vanilla extract
- 2 1/2 cups all-purpose flour
- 1 teaspoon baking soda
- 1/2 teaspoon salt
- 1 teaspoon pumpkin pie spice

Instructions

Make the Ice Cream:

In a medium bowl, whisk together the cream, milk, sugar, vanilla extract, pumpkin puree, and pumpkin pie spice until the sugar is completely dissolved.

Pour the mixture into the KitchenAid Ice Cream Attachment.

Churn on low speed for 25-30 minutes, or until the mixture reaches a soft-serve consistency.

Transfer the ice cream to a lidded container and freeze for at least 2 hours.

Make the Cookies:

Preheat the oven to 350°F (175°C).

In a large bowl, cream together the butter and sugars until light and fluffy. Beat in the eggs and vanilla until well combined.

In another bowl, whisk together the flour, baking soda, salt, and pumpkin pie spice. Gradually add the dry ingredients to the wet ingredients, mixing until just combined.

Drop tablespoon-sized balls of dough onto a baking sheet lined with parchment paper, spacing them about 2 inches apart. Flatten slightly with your hand.

Bake for 10-12 minutes, or until the edges are golden brown. Let cool completely.

Assemble the Sandwiches:

Scoop a generous amount of ice cream onto the flat side of one cookie. Top with another cookie, flat side down, and press gently to spread the ice cream evenly.

Wrap each sandwich in plastic wrap and freeze for at least 1 hour before serving.

Mocha Chip Ice Cream Sandwich

Servings: 8 sandwiches

Ingredients

For the Ice Cream:

- 2 cups heavy cream
- 1 cup whole milk
- 3/4 cup granulated sugar
- 1 teaspoon pure vanilla extract
- 2 tablespoons instant coffee granules
- 1/2 cup mini chocolate chips

For the Cookies:

- 1 cup unsalted butter, softened

- 1 cup granulated sugar
- 1 cup brown sugar, packed
- 2 large eggs
- 2 teaspoons pure vanilla extract
- 2 1/2 cups all-purpose flour
- 1/2 cup unsweetened cocoa powder
- 1 teaspoon baking soda
- 1/2 teaspoon salt

Instructions

Make the Ice Cream:

In a medium bowl, whisk together the cream, milk, sugar, vanilla extract, and instant coffee granules until the sugar is completely dissolved. Stir in the mini chocolate chips.

Pour the mixture into the KitchenAid Ice Cream Attachment.

Churn on low speed for 25-30 minutes, or until the mixture reaches a soft-serve consistency.

Transfer the ice cream to a lidded container and freeze for at least 2 hours.

Make the Cookies:

Preheat the oven to 350°F (175°C).

In a large bowl, cream together the butter and sugars until light and fluffy. Beat in the eggs and vanilla until well combined.

In another bowl, whisk together the flour, cocoa powder, baking soda, and salt. Gradually add the dry ingredients to the wet ingredients, mixing until just combined.

Drop tablespoon-sized balls of dough onto a baking sheet lined with parchment paper, spacing them about 2 inches apart. Flatten slightly with your hand.

Bake for 10-12 minutes, or until the edges are golden brown. Let cool completely.

Assemble the Sandwiches:

Scoop a generous amount of ice cream onto the flat side of one cookie. Top with another cookie, flat side down, and press gently to spread the ice cream evenly.

Wrap each sandwich in plastic wrap and freeze for at least 1 hour before serving.

Raspberry White Chocolate Chip Ice Cream Sandwich

Servings: 8 sandwiches

Ingredients

For the Ice Cream:

- 2 cups heavy cream
- 1 cup whole milk
- 3/4 cup granulated sugar
- 1 teaspoon pure vanilla extract
- 1 cup fresh raspberries
- 1/2 cup white chocolate chips

For the Cookies:

- 1 cup unsalted butter, softened
- 1 cup granulated sugar
- 1/2 cup brown sugar, packed
- 2 large eggs
- 2 teaspoons pure vanilla extract
- 2 1/2 cups all-purpose flour
- 1 teaspoon baking soda
- 1/2 teaspoon salt
- 1/2 cup freeze-dried raspberries, crushed
- 1 cup white chocolate chips

Instructions

Make the Ice Cream:

In a medium bowl, whisk together the cream, milk, sugar, and vanilla extract until the sugar is completely dissolved. Stir in the fresh raspberries and white chocolate chips.

Pour the mixture into the KitchenAid Ice Cream Attachment.

Churn on low speed for 25-30 minutes, or until the mixture reaches a soft-serve consistency.

Transfer the ice cream to a lidded container and freeze for at least 2 hours.

Make the Cookies:

Preheat the oven to 350°F (175°C).

In a large bowl, cream together the butter and sugars until light and fluffy. Beat in the eggs and vanilla until well combined.

In another bowl, whisk together the flour, baking soda, salt, and crushed freeze-dried raspberries. Gradually add the dry ingredients to the wet ingredients, mixing until just combined. Stir in the white chocolate chips.

Drop tablespoon-sized balls of dough onto a baking sheet lined with parchment paper, spacing them about 2 inches apart. Flatten slightly with your hand.

Bake for 10-12 minutes, or until the edges are golden brown. Let cool completely.

Assemble the Sandwiches:

Scoop a generous amount of ice cream onto the flat side of one cookie. Top with another cookie, flat side down, and press gently to spread the ice cream evenly.

Wrap each sandwich in plastic wrap and freeze for at least 1 hour before serving.

Pistachio Ice Cream Sandwich

Servings: 8 sandwiches

Ingredients

For the Ice Cream:

- 2 cups heavy cream
- 1 cup whole milk
- 3/4 cup granulated sugar
- 1 teaspoon pure vanilla extract
- 1/2 cup chopped pistachios

For the Cookies:

- 1 cup unsalted butter, softened
- 1 cup granulated sugar
- 1 cup brown sugar, packed
- 2 large eggs
- 2 teaspoons pure vanilla extract
- 2 1/2 cups all-purpose flour
- 1 teaspoon baking soda
- 1/2 teaspoon salt
- 1/2 cup finely chopped pistachios

Instructions

Make the Ice Cream:

In a medium bowl, whisk together the cream, milk, sugar, and vanilla extract until the sugar is completely dissolved. Stir in the chopped pistachios.

Pour the mixture into the KitchenAid Ice Cream Attachment.

Churn on low speed for 25-30 minutes, or until the mixture reaches a soft-serve consistency.

Transfer the ice cream to a lidded container and freeze for at least 2 hours.

Make the Cookies:

Preheat the oven to 350°F (175°C).

In a large bowl, cream together the butter and sugars until light and fluffy. Beat in the eggs and vanilla until well combined.

In another bowl, whisk together the flour, baking soda, salt, and finely chopped pistachios. Gradually add the dry ingredients to the wet ingredients, mixing until just combined.

Drop tablespoon-sized balls of dough onto a baking sheet lined with parchment paper, spacing them about 2 inches apart. Flatten slightly with your hand.

Bake for 10-12 minutes, or until the edges are golden brown. Let cool completely.

Assemble the Sandwiches:

Scoop a generous amount of ice cream onto the flat side of one cookie. Top with another cookie, flat side down, and press gently to spread the ice cream evenly.

Wrap each sandwich in plastic wrap and freeze for at least 1 hour before serving.

Lemon Blueberry Ice Cream Sandwich

Servings: 8 sandwiches

Ingredients

For the Ice Cream:

- 2 cups heavy cream
- 1 cup whole milk
- 3/4 cup granulated sugar
- 1 teaspoon pure vanilla extract
- 1/4 cup fresh lemon juice
- 1 tablespoon lemon zest
- 1/2 cup fresh blueberries

For the Cookies:

- 1 cup unsalted butter, softened
- 1 cup granulated sugar
- 1/2 cup brown sugar, packed
- 2 large eggs
- 2 teaspoons pure vanilla extract
- 2 1/2 cups all-purpose flour
- 1 teaspoon baking soda
- 1/2 teaspoon salt
- 1 tablespoon lemon zest
- 1/2 cup dried blueberries

Instructions

Make the Ice Cream:

In a medium bowl, whisk together the cream, milk, sugar, vanilla extract, lemon juice, and lemon zest until the sugar is completely dissolved. Stir in the fresh blueberries.

Pour the mixture into the KitchenAid Ice Cream Attachment.

Churn on low speed for 25-30 minutes, or until the mixture reaches a soft-serve consistency.

Transfer the ice cream to a lidded container and freeze for at least 2 hours.

Make the Cookies:

Preheat the oven to 350°F (175°C).

In a large bowl, cream together the butter and sugars until light and fluffy. Beat in the eggs and vanilla until well combined.

In another bowl, whisk together the flour, baking soda, salt, and lemon zest. Gradually add the dry ingredients to the wet ingredients, mixing until just combined. Stir in the dried blueberries.

Drop tablespoon-sized balls of dough onto a baking sheet lined with parchment paper, spacing them about 2 inches apart. Flatten slightly with your hand.

Bake for 10-12 minutes, or until the edges are golden brown. Let cool completely.

Assemble the Sandwiches:

Scoop a generous amount of ice cream onto the flat side of one cookie. Top with another cookie, flat side down, and press gently to spread the ice cream evenly.

Wrap each sandwich in plastic wrap and freeze for at least 1 hour before serving.

Peanut Butter Chocolate Ice Cream Sandwich

Servings: 8 sandwiches

Ingredients

For the Ice Cream:

- 2 cups heavy cream
- 1 cup whole milk
- 3/4 cup granulated sugar
- 1 teaspoon pure vanilla extract
- 1/2 cup creamy peanut butter
- 1/2 cup mini chocolate chips

For the Cookies:

- 1 cup unsalted butter, softened
- 1 cup granulated sugar
- 1 cup brown sugar, packed
- 2 large eggs
- 2 teaspoons pure vanilla extract
- 2 1/2 cups all-purpose flour
- 1/2 cup unsweetened cocoa powder
- 1 teaspoon baking soda
- 1/2 teaspoon salt

Instructions

Make the Ice Cream:

In a medium bowl, whisk together the cream, milk, sugar, vanilla extract, and peanut butter until the sugar is completely dissolved. Stir in the mini chocolate chips.

Pour the mixture into the KitchenAid Ice Cream Attachment.

Churn on low speed for 25-30 minutes, or until the mixture reaches a soft-serve consistency.

Transfer the ice cream to a lidded container and freeze for at least 2 hours.

Make the Cookies:

Preheat the oven to 350°F (175°C).

In a large bowl, cream together the butter and sugars until light and fluffy. Beat in the eggs and vanilla until well combined.

In another bowl, whisk together the flour, cocoa powder, baking soda, and salt. Gradually add the dry ingredients to the wet ingredients, mixing until just combined.

Drop tablespoon-sized balls of dough onto a baking sheet lined with parchment paper, spacing them about 2 inches apart. Flatten slightly with your hand.

Bake for 10-12 minutes, or until the edges are golden brown. Let cool completely.

Assemble the Sandwiches:

Scoop a generous amount of ice cream onto the flat side of one cookie. Top with another cookie, flat side down, and press gently to spread the ice cream evenly.

Wrap each sandwich in plastic wrap and freeze for at least 1 hour before serving.

Cherry Garcia Ice Cream Sandwich

Servings: 8 sandwiches

Ingredients

For the Ice Cream:

- 2 cups heavy cream
- 1 cup whole milk
- 3/4 cup granulated sugar
- 1 teaspoon pure vanilla extract
- 1 cup chopped fresh cherries
- 1/2 cup chopped dark chocolate

For the Cookies:

- 1 cup unsalted butter, softened
- 1 cup granulated sugar
- 1 cup brown sugar, packed
- 2 large eggs
- 2 teaspoons pure vanilla extract
- 2 1/2 cups all-purpose flour
- 1 teaspoon baking soda
- 1/2 teaspoon salt
- 1/2 cup chopped dried cherries
- 1 cup dark chocolate chips

Instructions

Make the Ice Cream:

In a medium bowl, whisk together the cream, milk, sugar, and vanilla extract until the sugar is completely dissolved. Stir in the chopped fresh cherries and dark chocolate.

Pour the mixture into the KitchenAid Ice Cream Attachment.

Churn on low speed for 25-30 minutes, or until the mixture reaches a soft-serve consistency.

Transfer the ice cream to a lidded container and freeze for at least 2 hours.

Make the Cookies:

Preheat the oven to 350°F (175°C).

In a large bowl, cream together the butter and sugars until light and fluffy. Beat in the eggs and vanilla until well combined.

In another bowl, whisk together the flour, baking soda, and salt. Gradually add the dry ingredients to the wet ingredients, mixing until just combined. Stir in the dried cherries and dark chocolate chips.

Drop tablespoon-sized balls of dough onto a baking sheet lined with parchment paper, spacing them about 2 inches apart. Flatten slightly with your hand.

Bake for 10-12 minutes, or until the edges are golden brown. Let cool completely.

Assemble the Sandwiches:

Scoop a generous amount of ice cream onto the flat side of one cookie. Top with another cookie, flat side down, and press gently to spread the ice cream evenly.

Wrap each sandwich in plastic wrap and freeze for at least 1 hour before serving.

8. Toppings and Mix-Ins

Chocolate Chips

Description: Small pieces of chocolate that can be mixed into the ice cream base or sprinkled on top.

Usage: Add 1/2 cup of chocolate chips to the ice cream base during the last 5 minutes of churning or sprinkle on top before serving.

Caramel Sauce

Description: A sweet, sticky sauce made from caramelized sugar, butter, and cream.

Usage: Drizzle 1/4 cup of caramel sauce over the ice cream before serving, or swirl it into the ice cream base during the last few minutes of churning.

Crushed Cookies

Description: Crumbled pieces of cookies, such as Oreos or chocolate chip cookies.

Usage: Fold 1 cup of crushed cookies into the ice cream base after churning, or sprinkle on top before serving.

Fresh Fruit

Description: Sliced or diced fresh fruit, such as strawberries, blueberries, or bananas.

Usage: Add 1 cup of fresh fruit to the ice cream base during the last 5 minutes of churning, or use as a topping before serving.

Nuts

Description: Chopped nuts, such as almonds, walnuts, or pecans.

Usage: Mix 1/2 cup of chopped nuts into the ice cream base during the last 5 minutes of churning, or sprinkle on top before serving.

Marshmallows

Description: Small, soft, and fluffy confections.

Usage: Fold 1 cup of mini marshmallows into the ice cream base after churning, or use as a topping before serving.

Sprinkles

Description: Small, colorful pieces of sugar candy.

Usage: Mix 1/4 cup of sprinkles into the ice cream base during the last 5 minutes of churning, or sprinkle on top before serving.

Brownie Bites

Description: Small chunks of brownies.

Usage: Fold 1 cup of brownie bites into the ice cream base after churning, or use as a topping before serving.

Coconut Flakes

Description: Shredded or flaked dried coconut.

Usage: Mix 1/2 cup of coconut flakes into the ice cream base during the last 5 minutes of churning, or sprinkle on top before serving.

Graham Cracker Crumbs

Description: Crushed graham crackers.

Usage: Fold 1 cup of graham cracker crumbs into the ice cream base after churning, or use as a topping before serving.

Hot Fudge Sauce

Description: A rich, thick chocolate sauce, typically served warm.

Usage: Drizzle 1/4 cup of hot fudge sauce over the ice cream before serving, or swirl it into the ice cream base during the last few minutes of churning.

Toffee Bits

Description: Small, crunchy pieces of toffee.

Usage: Mix 1/2 cup of toffee bits into the ice cream base during the last 5 minutes of churning, or sprinkle on top before serving.

Peanut Butter Swirl

Description: Creamy peanut butter mixed into the ice cream base.

Usage: Add 1/4 cup of melted peanut butter to the ice cream base during the last few minutes of churning, creating a swirl effect.

Chocolate-Covered Pretzels

Description: Crunchy pretzels coated in chocolate.

Usage: Fold 1 cup of chopped chocolate-covered pretzels into the ice cream base after churning, or use as a topping before serving.

Candied Ginger

Description: Small pieces of ginger that have been cooked in sugar syrup and dried, adding a sweet and spicy flavor.

Usage: Mix 1/4 cup of finely chopped candied ginger into the ice cream base during the last 5 minutes of churning, or sprinkle on top before serving.

Conclusion

Making homemade ice cream is a delightful and rewarding experience that brings joy to any occasion. With the KitchenAid Ice Cream Maker Attachment, you have the perfect tool to create a wide variety of delicious and unique frozen treats right in your own kitchen. From classic flavors to innovative new combinations, this recipe book has guided you through an exciting journey of ice cream making.

By now, you've mastered the essential techniques, from preparing the perfect base to churning and freezing your ice cream to perfection. You've explored different categories, including classic favorites, gourmet and unique flavors, dairy-free and vegan options, refreshing sorbets and gelatos, indulgent alcohol-infused ice creams, and creative ice cream sandwiches and treats.

I hope this recipe book has inspired you to embrace the art of homemade ice cream making. Whether you're crafting a simple vanilla for a family gathering or experimenting with exotic flavors for a special treat, the joy of creating your own ice cream is unmatched.

Happy churning!

Metric Conversion Chart

U.S. Customary System	Metric System
VOLUME	
¼ teaspoon	1.2 milliliters
½ teaspoon	2.5 milliliters
1 teaspoon	5 milliliters
1 tablespoon	15 milliliters
¼ cup	60 milliliters
⅓ cup	80 milliliters
½ cup	120 milliliters
⅔ cup	160 milliliters
¾ cup	175 milliliters
1 cup	240 milliliters
MASS (WEIGHT)	
4 ounces	110 grams
8 ounces	224 grams
12 ounces	340 grams
16 ounces	455 grams

U.S. Customary System		Metric System	
TEMPERATURE			
Fahrenheit		**Celsius**	
350 degrees		180 degrees	
375 degrees		190 degrees	
400 degrees		200 degrees	
425 degrees		220 degrees	
LENGTH			
⅛ inch		0.3	centimeter
¼ inch		0.6	centimeter
½ inch		1.25	centimeters
1 inch		2.5	centimeters
2 inches		5	centimeters
6 inches		15	centimeters
9 inches		23	centimeters
9 × 13 inches	23 × 33		centimeters
12 inches		30.5	centimeters

About the Author

Jessie Mohr is a culinary enthusiast and self-taught ice cream aficionado with a passion for creating delicious, homemade desserts. With over a decade of experience experimenting in the kitchen, Jessie has mastered the art of ice cream making, turning simple ingredients into delightful and unique frozen treats. Her love for food and creativity shines through in her recipes, which are known for their innovative flavors and approachable techniques.

Recipe Index